also from

aplomb publishing
San Francisco

Movie Star & the Mobster

Who Nuked The Duke?

What Ever Happened to Mommie Dearest?

Alfred Hitchcock: The Icon Years

Reel Horror - True Horrors Behind Hollywood's Scary Movies

Curse of the Silver Screen - Tragedy & Disaster Behind the Movies

Master of Disaster - Irwin Allen: The Disaster Years

www.aplombpublishing.com

The Lost Hitchcocks

By John William Law

aplomb publishing
San Francisco

The Lost Hitchcocks

Published by Aplomb Publishing, San Francisco, California.
Copyright 2018.

ISBN: 978-0-9892475-6-6

1st edition

Manufactured in the United States of America.

No part of this publication may be reprinted without written permission from the publisher. For more information, write Aplomb Publishing, editor@aplombpublishing.com.

Dedicated to Alfred Hitchcock fans.

"In the old days villains had moustaches and kicked the dog. Audiences are smarter today. They don't want their villain to be thrown at them with green limelight his face. They want an ordinary human being with failings."

- Alfred Hitchcock

Table of Contents

-	Acknowledgements	Page 13
-	Preface	Page 15
1	Introduction	Page 21
2	The Formative Years	Page 29
3	Titanic	Page 39
4	The Lodger	Page 51
5	Greenmantle	Page 61
6	Flamingo Feather	Page 69
7	Hamlet	Page 81
8	The Bramble Bush	Page 91
9	The Wreck of the Mary Deare	Page 101
10	No Bail for the Judge	Page 111
11	Thunderball	Page 123
12	The Blind Man	Page 133
13	Mary Rose	Page 145
14	The Three Hostages	Page 179
15	Kaleidoscope	Page 187
16	Jaws	Page 201
17	The Short Night	Page 211
18	Death of the Master	Page 219
19	Made Without Hitch	Page 227
20	Closing Remarks	Page 235

Appendix

Filmography	Page 246
Sources	Page 253
Index	Page 263

THE LOST HITCHCOCKS

Acknowledgements

Thank you to David Young for proofreading and editing support, and to Thomas Moulton for assistance with the cover design. In addition, special thanks to the Motion Picture Academy of Arts and Science and the Margaret Herrick Library for access to resources that helped make this book possible.

THE LOST HITCHCOCKS

preface

THE LOST HITCHCOCKS

"I don't want to film a "slice of life" because people can get that at home, in the street, or even in front of the movie theater. They don't have to pay money to see a slice of life."

- Alfred Hitchcock

Opening Remarks

Many years ago a small publisher asked if I was interested in doing a biography on Alfred Hitchcock. At the time I had submitted a draft concept for a book on another filmmaker to the publisher to see if they were interested in my idea. It was a book on a lesser-known filmmaker and something I had been researching. They rejected my proposal, but ask instead if I'd be interested in doing a book on the life of the master of suspense.

THE LOST HITCHCOCKS

Having been a fan of Alfred Hitchcock's for many years the idea intrigued me and I told them I had a few ideas that might interest them relating to the director. I suggested a book that looked at the more comedic side of the director, or one that centered on the cool, but tragic blonde that was found in so many of his films. Their response was that I had misunderstood their inquiry. They actually wanted "a biography" on the life of Alfred Hitchcock.

I said there were so many excellent biographies already written about the famed director that I didn't think I could add anything new to the subject. Ultimately I decided it wasn't something I'd be interested in pursuing. To produce such a book could take years out of a person's life, and it probably wouldn't result in anything better than what had been done before.

I ultimately passed on the idea and the correspondence with the publisher ended there. I never did find out if they got the book they were looking for and I moved onto other projects.

Some years later, in between projects, I got an idea for a book on Alfred Hitchcock that focused on his later films – the years following *Psycho* – and how that one film cast a giant shadow over the director and his work. While a crowning achievement in cinema, for the man that made it, *Psycho* became a hard act to follow.

The book, *Alfred Hitchcock: The Icon Years* was released in 2010, in time for *Psycho*'s 50th anniversary and became the Hitchcock book I never expected to write. I was honored when the title was named Best Non-Fiction Biography in 2011 by a book readers association.

In 2012, because of my book on Hitchcock, I was invited to appear on camera in a film documentary about the making of *The Birds*. The film, *Hitchcock's Monster Movie*, is featured on a bonus disc in Universal Studios first release of a master collection of Hitchcock's most loved classics on Blu-ray and on the official Blu-ray release of *The Birds* in 2014.

My association with the master of suspense might have ended there, but the success of the book and the interest in Hitchcock got me to thinking about all the work he never completed. I had included references to several of the films in my earlier book and began compiling a longer list of failed films that might make an interesting collection for a follow-up book on Hitchcock. Hitchcock once said, "The secret of motion picture suspense is to keep audiences in a state of 'pleasurable anxiety.'"

If Hitchcock determined he would be unable to deliver on his recipe for suspense, he'd abandon a project. His aim, he said was, "Make audiences suffer in their soft, comfortable seats as they see characters of the drama grope for solutions which they, the audience, already know."

Hitchcock, like most prolific and successful directors, was approached with many stories, screenplays, novels, and scripts. He had the luxury of picking and choosing his projects. He was also an avid reader and theatergoer who found his film ideas in many likely and unlikely places. Plays, short stories, newspaper clippings, magazine articles and more could spark an idea. Other writers, agents, producers and actors also found stories and screenplays they felt were perfect for the director and suggested them to him. He received many such offers, but would be forced to reject the majority in order to create the gems he actually left us with. While some received a passing glance or brief consideration, others were more seriously considered, with some actually entering various stages of pre-production.

With that, I present *The Lost Hitchcocks*, a look at a collection of the most interesting films the master of suspense intended to make, but ultimately dropped for one reason or another. In some cases, these films represent a lost opportunity, replaced by a film that may or may not have resulted in a classic movie. In every case, the story behind the film offers a fascinating glimpse behind the man, his thought process and the movie industry he dedicated much of his life to.

- John William Law

The Master of Suspense, Alfred Hitchcock, in his prime.

one

THE LOST HITCHCOCKS

"Making a film means, first of all, to tell a story. That story can be an improbable one, but it should never be banal. It must be dramatic and human. What is drama, after all, but life with the dull bits cut out."

- Alfred Hitchcock

Introduction

  In 2012, critics named *Vertigo* the best film of all time. In the film poll conducted every 10 years by *Sight and Sound Magazine*, 846 critics and 358 directors weighed in on the greatest films of all time. Alfred Hitchcock's 1958 masterpiece, which at one time had been panned by critics, and not regarded a financially successful film, moved up from the number two spot in 2002 to replace *Citizen Kane*. In fact, it was the first time that *Citizen Kane* didn't top the list since 1952.

Also in 2012, Anthony Hopkins graced the big screen as Sir Alfred Hitchcock in the first biopic on the life and work of the famed director. Focusing on the production of his most successful film *Psycho*, *Hitchcock*, the film, would garner one Oscar nomination as well as nominations for a Golden Globe and two BAFTA nominations.

The Girl, a 2012 television movie about the troubled relationship between Hitchcock and Tippi Hedren was distributed by HBO and the BBC, giving viewers another look inside the life and mind of the master of suspense.

Hitch on the cover of 'Life' magazine in 1963.

Then in 2013, American television audiences were graced with *Bates Motel*, a series looking back at the formation of the young Norman Bates, borrowing heavily from Hitchcock's *Psycho* to make audience squirm and take notice.

Along with these new projects centering on the world's most famous director, 2012 also saw the release of a Blu-ray box set of some of his most relevant works. *The Masterpiece Collection* featured many of his major hits of the last 30 years of his career, along with a brand new documentary, *Hitchcock's Monster Movie*, a glimpse at the director's work, *The Birds*. Then, in 2015, *Hitchcock/Truffaut* was released as a documentary discussing the work of Hitch through a series of interviews he gave in the 1960s for the book, *Cinema According to Hitchcock*, released in 1966. In 2017, *North by Northwest* was released in select cities through Fathom Events.

The fact that Alfred Hitchcock remains relevant to critics, moviemakers and the movie-going public at large is surprising only in that his death was more than 35 years ago. His presence is still felt on the big screen and nearly all aspects of filmmaking. It's one of the many reasons we continue to read, research and write about his contributions to film and his impact on the medium itself.

One of the other interesting things about Hitchcock was the detail in which he crafted his films and the collection of material that remains. The storyboards, notes, audio recordings and records associated with his filmmaking process provide a wealth of rich details about his plans and reasoning behind the movies he made – and the movies he did not. He dedicated much of his life to making films and desired to be remembered for his contributions as an artist. Documenting much of his thought processes, his work ethic, and the ideas and themes behind his work, provides a rich layer of information, allowing us to peel away Hitchcock's work, like an onion, to reveal a much deeper side of him.

In a career that spanned some sixty years, seven decades and more than 50 feature films, he was also well known for the TV series bearing his name, that ran on two networks for 10 years. He was welcomed into America's homes with a long-running mystery magazine, a host of paperback books telling "Hitchcockian" tales, record albums of his movie scores, and even a board game.

With so much product created under the brand of Alfred Hitch-

Hitchcock at his peak in the early 1960s.

cock, it stands to reason that he wouldn't complete every project he set out to. Most successful filmmakers have a roster of films they failed to complete. The fact that Hitchcock has a list is no surprise. The challenge of financing, scripting, casting, filming and releasing a movie can be so daunting it's sometime surprising that as many films see the light of day that do.

However, with Hitchcock, the fascination with his career has obviously been spent on the critical and financially successful films he released. His less successful works have been relegated to briefer detail, and his unfinished works have often been left behind entirely. However, these unrealized efforts often offer equally fascinating tales behind the man who attempted to make them and those that worked alongside him. The fact that they were left incomplete leaves us with a mystery worthy of the master's work itself. What could have been? How would these features have changed his career and the lives of those who might have helped him complete them? Would they have been hits or failures?

Some of the films Hitchcock planned on doing, or seriously considered making, were ultimately made by other directors. Several were even hits at the box office. Even so, the incomplete works of Alfred Hitchcock have as much to say about the man and the director as those he completed. In some cases, these projects shed more light on his challenges and difficulties, and his idea of what makes or does not make a successful film, than his completed works. As one of the most successful and powerful men in Hollywood, even Hitchcock knew when to call it quits and move on.

THE LOST HITCHCOCKS

two

THE LOST HITCHCOCKS

"I come from a Catholic family, and I had a strict, religious upbringing. My wife converted to Catholicism before our marriage. I don't think I can be labeled a Catholic artist, but it may be that one's upbringing influences a man's life and guides his instinct."

- Alfred Hitchcock

A Legend Takes Shape

Personality traits are defined as stable dimensions of an individual's personality. They not only influence our thinking, they drive our behavior in many situations. For people who are described as obese – or those that struggle with weight throughout their lives – studies have found a variety of common personality traits. While the science is speculative, it suggests that people suffering from obesity are less social and are more prone to bouts of anxiety than people not characterized as obese. While it is widely accepted that they struggle with low self-esteem, people who are overweight are often more likely to suffer from depression and mood disorders.

Heavyset from the time he was very young, it was a condition that would plague Alfred Hitchcock his entire life, making him increasingly shy and reclusive. In many ways it became a foundation on which much of his personality was formed and it is through his personality that we get an understanding of not only what drove his career, but his life. It would determine the choices he would make and the directions he would take throughout his life.

Many have described Hitchcock as an emotionally volatile personality. Though often not exhibiting the highs, he could quickly shut down and avoid people or difficult situations. He would abandon relationships with those around him and people often found it hard to understand what they had done to displease him.

Another common trait found in many people who struggle with their weight is self-discipline. It's suggested that difficulties in maintaining diets or good eating habits often lead to life-long struggles with weight, and for Hitchcock, this would certainly be true. His weight varied widely throughout much of his life. While he was never considered a slim man, his size went from large to rotund. In periods of his greatest productivity he could swing widely on the weight scale.

One might suggest that his personality trait of struggling to stick with his diet could also be a factor in his ability to stick with a difficult film project. As a prolific film director it can easily be argued that Hitchcock's success illustrates a strong discipline and focus on his career, but at the same time he had a vast number of films that went unfinished. He'd often acquire a story or concept for a film and dive full-force into the details only to abandon the project once some challenge or difficultly arose that he couldn't easily find his way around. This was a common thread through much of his career.

The Formative Years

Born August 13, 1899 in Leytonstone, London, Alfred was the second and youngest son of William and Emma Jane Hitchcock. He also had an older sister. His childhood has been described as both lonely and

Young Alfred Hitchcock first established himself as a promising filmmaker in Britain in the 1920s.

sheltered. He claimed that as a young boy he was sent by his father to the local police station with a note asking the officer to lock him in a cell as punishment for bad behavior. While it was only a short span of about five or ten minutes, Hitchcock never forgot the incident and harbored a lifelong fear of policemen and incarceration. He would include many such references in his films. His father would die when he was 14 and that event, as well, would also have an impact on the characters and stories of his future projects.

After graduating from school, he became a draftsman and advertising designer, but his interest in photography lead him to work with a film production company in London.

He obtained a full-time job at Islington Studios designing movie titles for silent films in 1920. Over the next several years he would explore numerous other avenues in the film business until 1925 when he began directing silent movies.

In December 1926 he married his assistant director, Alma Reville and their only child, a daughter named Patricia, was born in July 1928. By the 1930s, with experience, his skill improved, and by the end of the decade he had become one of the most successful filmmakers in the United Kingdom. Soon Hollywood came calling.

In 1939, David O. Selznick signed Hitchcock to a seven-year contract and the director relocated to Los Angeles with his family and began what would be a very prolific, but, at times, difficult period for Hitchcock. While thrilled to be able to make big budget motion pictures that masses of moviegoers could enjoy, Hitchcock was often frustrated by Selznick's struggle for creative control over his films. However, out of the struggle for power, Hitchcock would create some of his most memorable and challenging films. It was during this period that he, with the help of Selznick would direct the Oscar-winning *Rebecca* in 1940. While the film earned the Academy Award for Best Picture of 1940 for Selznick, Hitchcock was denied the Best Director award. But he would go on to direct numerous other notable classics of the decade, including *Suspicion* (1941), *Saboteur* (1942), *Shadow of a Doubt* (1943), *Lifeboat*

(1944) and *Notorious* (1946).

He also had some notable failures during this time that prevented him from being viewed as Hollywood's golden boy. Lackluster response to films like *The Paradine Case* (1947) and *Under Capricorn* (1949) would frustrate Hitchcock and he would blame others for preventing him from achieving his cinematic goal. He would later seek out opportunities to produce his own films, in his later years, in order to retain as much creative control as possible.

With the 1950s he would produce many of his most recognizable works, including *Strangers on a Train* (1951), *Rear Window* (1954), *Dial M for Murder* (1954), *Vertigo* (1958) and *North by Northwest* (1959). However, as in the 1940s, he would have several missteps with disappointing releases in *Stage Fright* (1950) and *The Wrong Man* (1957).

Hitchcock would also move into the world of television with his TV series *Alfred Hitchcock Presents* in 1955 and lend his name to a successful series of paperback books that carried the trademark tales of suspense and macabre that would make his television show a success with viewers for a decade.

With roughly 30 years of film experience behind him, his name would draw attention to the relatively new medium of television drama. Once it did, his face became better known than many of his actors. Although he only directed 17 half-hour or hour-long episodes of his show, the series would air some 350 episodes, and like his books, he would be putting his face on every episode, almost stamping the work of others as his own. It was his style and his show. One of the trademarks of the series was the iconic Hitchcock silhouette, which reportedly came from a sketch used for a Christmas card designed by Hitchcock.

The show would do quite well in the ratings during its first few seasons, moving between fourth and sixth place, behind staples like *The Ed Sullivan Show* and *Lucy*. In its second season the series would earn an Emmy Award for writing. The TV series would also prove financially rewarding. Hitchcock's contract would earn him more than $125,000 per show, as well as all rights of sale and rebroadcast after each show first aired. For production he set up a television company, Shamley Productions, named after a summer home he and his wife purchased in Shamley Green, a small village south of London, back in 1928. Hitch's contract with his sponsor, Bristol-Meyers, stipulated that he would only direct an "unspecified number of episodes" each season, allowing him to continue to focus on his feature films.

His TV series aired on CBS from 1955 until 1960, when it was picked up by NBC in 1960. After two seasons on NBC, CBS brought the show back to its network, but this time as an hour-long show and renaming it *The Alfred Hitchcock Hour*. Its final season, in 1964, would be on NBC, also in an hour-long format.

His television work allowed him to work with a planned schedule - something his film actors would grow accustomed to when working on his later movies. He ended his day at 4 p.m. and enjoyed the regularity of a schedule. His half-hour dramas were filmed in three days and the hour-long shows in five. Even though he didn't direct the bulk of the shows his mark was left on each. He selected each show that would be filmed and oversaw many key production decisions. He would even employ many members of his TV crew on future film work and a number of the actors in his shows would find their way into his films.

During his years in television he continued to work in film, directing many of his most profitable and memorable films. *North by Northwest, Psycho, The Birds, Frenzy* and *Family Plot,* among the best, while films like *Marnie, Torn Curtain* and *Topaz* left critics and moviegoers wondering what went wrong.

It was his personality, his name, and his face on the movie screen, the TV screen and in bookstores, that presented the Hitchcock brand of macabre suspense. He was offered many scripts, short stories, books and other story ideas for potential episodes of his TV series, or for a film. His name and face carried the clout to get projects off the ground, but as a filmmaker, Hitchcock had to have a vision for the stories he would tell and that vision would have to become something he knew – or at least believed – he could realize. Oftentimes, projects started off with the greatest of expectations, but would fall apart as he tried to weave them together through the eye of a camera. While we're left with a magnificent collection of completed masterpieces and studies in suspense, left behind is a collection of near misses, or what could have been films from the master of suspense.

THE LOST HITCHCOCKS

three

THE LOST HITCHCOCKS

"To make a fine film, you need three things ... a great script, a great script, and a great script."

– **Alfred Hitchcock**

Abandon Sinking Ship

"While we were shooting T*he Lady Vanishes*, I got a cable from Selznick, asking me to come to Hollywood to direct a picture based on the sinking of the *Titanic*," recalled Hitchcock. "As soon as I had finished work on *The Lady Vanishes*, I went to America for the first time and stayed there for ten days. That was in August of 1937. I agreed to do the picture about the *Titanic*, but since the contract with Selznick wasn't due to start until April, 1939, I had time to make another British film, and that was *Jamaica Inn*."

THE LOST HITCHCOCKS

Movie historians suggest that it was a foregone conclusion that Alfred Hitchcock was destined to make his way to America to make movies in Hollywood. As a big fish in a small pond in the United Kingdom, his talents could never fully be exploited there as they could in Hollywood with major financing, large-scale productions and first-rate casts and crews. It was always expected that Hitchcock would be drawn to the big movie studios of Los Angeles. He only had to decide when – and with whom he would work.

Hitchcock already had a strong association with American film production. "I'm American trained," he once said. "My first work was at the Paramount Studios in London – then it was Famous Players Lasky. All of the personnel at the studio were American, and as soon as you entered the studio doors you were in an American atmosphere. I started out as a designer of titles working with Mordant Hall, who was a critic later for *The New York Times*, and for Tom Geraghty, who had been a writer for Douglas Fairbanks."

After years in Britain, a young Hitchcock was lured to Hollywood.

David O. Selznick, by the end of the 1930s, had wined and dined Hitchcock to come to work for Selznick International and Hitchcock seemed happy with the idea, provided the terms of his employment and the selection of the appropriate picture could be worked out. In the summer of 1938, contracts were signed and Hitchcock had set his sights on a big screen version of *Rebecca,* a torrid romance and mystery novel by Daphne Du Maurier. Hitchcock had read the galley proofs and thought it would make a splendid film. He'd hoped to purchase the film rights, but the cost was a bit out of his reach.

Working for Selznick would allow Hitchcock access and opportunity in Hollywood that he would never enjoy by himself, but he would have to deal with a powerful producer who had strong ideas about properties, stars and even the direction of his motion pictures. Hitchcock respected that dedication to the craft. "If I do go to Hollywood," Hitchcock told one reporter, "I'd only work for Selznick."

While Hitchcock still had hopes for directing *Rebecca*, Selznick approached him with the idea of another film to kick of his Hollywood directing career. In a telegram to his agents in May 1938 Selznick inquired if, "Hitchcock was free to come to California in mid-August to direct a film version of "The Titanic."

Based on a story by Wilson Mizner and Carl Harbraugh, Selznick hoped to lure Hitchcock to Hollywood to begin crafting the film treatment as soon as possible. Because the original story centered on the romance of a couple, Selznick knew the film version would require significant reworking to add in the suspense and visual effects to draw in viewers. Selznick asked Hitchcock if knew of any screenwriters who might be up to the task of completing the necessary screenplay. He wanted to waste no time on the film adaptation because he knew the screenplay would take some time produce into a successful picture grand enough to tell *Titanic*'s tale.

With Hitchcock having the freedom to name the writer, Selznick included in the telegram that, "filming could be underway by mid-August." Though the producer did cover himself. If he wasn't happy with the screenplay, noting, "Please discuss this frankly and thoroughly with him [the writer] making doubly sure that there will be no disappointment if I should decide against it."

Hitchcock accepted Selznick's terms, knowing that a Hollywood production would allow him the opportunity to make a human drama on a big budget scale. The director responded to Selznick via telegram that he had, "very good ideas on subject and had contemplated doing roughly the same thing himself."

Selznick floated a fantastic concept Hitchcock's way when he suggest using a real ship for filming the sinking. The producer wanted to purchase a massive old ship named the *Leviathan* that was sitting in a ship yard and restore the ship to make it resemble the *Titanic*. He then planned to tow it to a location where they could then sink the ship and capture it on film. Hitchcock imagined the fantastic scene of capturing the sinking as the ship fell into the sea and lost all power, disappearing below the horizon.

In Britain, the Cunard Line, makers of Titanic, raised some concerns over the idea of a major motion picture retelling of the tale. Fearing

the tragedy could impact potential cruise travel, Hitchcock assured them his film would not. "Out of the Titanic disaster," he said, "had developed the iceberg patrol system, the requirement that every ship carry wireless equipment, a dozen other safety measures."

Hitch convinced Cunard executives that his film would only make cruise travelers feel safer. "Over the grave of the Titanic rides, in safety, the *Queen Mary*," he assured them, would be the message his film delivered.

Hitchcock promised Selznick he could make himself available to the producer within two weeks. However, Hitchcock told Selznick that August would be, "too soon to have a suitable screenplay," ready to kick off production. The script would take months to craft and Selznick ultimately agreed he was overly optimistic in his earlier telegram.

When it came time to negotiate a deal, Hitchcock asked for $50,000 in exchange for one picture over a six-month timetable. In addition, he wanted round-trip travel and accommodations for himself and his wife. Selznick rejected his terms, unwilling to offer that much money for a single film over a six-month period. Hitchcock was willing to accept $50,000 for the first year of work, provided the salary was raised to $75,000 in the second year. He also wanted the ability to approve his own assignments, as well as any projects he might be loaned out to do for another studio by the producer.

Hitchcock, however, still optimistic about the idea of *Titanic*, announced he would come to Hollywood at his own expense the week after completing his current film, *The Lady Vanishes*. Because Selznick wasn't footing the bill, Hitchcock told the press he would be meeting with David O. Selznick "and other producers," as he considered the future of his film career in America.

Sailing on the *Queen Mary* during the last week of May 1938, Alfred and Alma arrived in New York on June 6. They initially told the press they were there working on a script called "False Witness" and kept talk of *Titanic* out of the papers. New York talent agent Katharine "Kay" Brown met them at the dock. Brown worked for Selznick and reportedly was the one who suggested Margaret Mitchell's *Gone With the Wind* to Selznick as a potential film. Selznick would accept her idea and dedicate a large amount of money and time toward the epic, reaping rewards after its release.

Hitchcock, interviewed in July 1938, told *The New York Times* that the script for *Titanic* was incomplete, but he had definite ideas about the story. When asked for details on the story, he joked, "Quite obvious what the last two reels will be. Beyond that nothing."

David O. Selznick orchestrated Hitchcock's arrival in Hollywood.

The director explained to the journalist, "Everyone in the world knows what is going to happen to the Titanic. The question is 'when?' There's your suspense. 'When?' It's better that way. Look at *Mutiny on the Bounty*, if it had been called 'The Jolly Old Bounty' or 'Rovers on the Bounty,' audiences would have become restless during the early reels. They'd have been wondering why all this repetition of scenes showing the brutality of the captain, the resentment of officers and crew. But 'Mutiny' on the Bounty – they knew what was coming, but they didn't know when. There was your suspense."

Reports suggest that it was unlikely that David O. Selznick would kick off a Hitchcock picture until after he completed work on *Gone With the Wind*, but Hitchcock, on the other hand, was eager to get to work immediately and urged Selznick to make a deal. Hitchcock kept his options open by meeting with Samuel Goldwyn, hoping it might persuade Selznick to get him under contract, rather losing him to MGM.

Selznick, however, shocked Hitchcock by suggesting he take the MGM deal, believing it might actually be more beneficial to both, allowing Hitch to get to America more quickly and he could still work with Selznick, but simply on loan from MGM.

In reality, most of Hollywood expected Hitchcock would work for Selznick and the other offers were unrealistic. In addition to MGM, the director met with Adolph Zukor at Paramount and executives at both RKO and Warner Bros. One Hollywood memo noted that Hitchcock was to, "hold off on discussion until they finish with David O. Selznick.

Three weeks after arriving in America, Hitchcock was still without a deal. By the end of June the director was growing frustrated, complaining to his Beverly Hills agency about Selznick's indecision, saying he'd rather be simply told "no," than go on waiting for an offer that might never arrive.

Finally, on July 2 events turned in Hitchcock's favor when he received an offer, but it wasn't exactly the offer he had been waiting for. The offer consisted of the agreed Selznick-Hitchcock picture, preliminarily named "Titanic," but Selznick stated he had the ability to "substitute any other film." The deal also stipulated that Hitchcock would make four additional films for Selznick International over the next four years.

The Selznick contract would keep Hitchcock obligated to the producer until 1943, but, on the upside, he could be loaned out to other studios for other projects. The contract would begin sometime between January and April of 1939. While it was agreed his salary for the first film would be $50,000, he wouldn't see a raise to $75,000 until completion of the additional four films. Not quite the deal Hitchcock had hoped for. However, additional expenses for relocation for Hitchcock, as well as salary and relocation costs for his assistant, Joan Harrison, were included in the final deal.

To the surprise of some, by the time the final contract was written and signed, no mention of *Titanic* was included in the language, leading film historians to believe that by July 1938, Selznick had lost interest in the idea of a major motion picture on the sinking of the infamous ocean liner. His fantastic idea of sinking an ocean liner fell through when the asking price to purchase the *Leviathan* was $848,000, and far above what he could afford.

While Hitchcock was not thrilled with the offer he was convinced that the prestige of working for Selznick International would only increase his income on loan-outs to other studios and his value in Hollywood for future contracts. Hitchcock accepted the offer on July 6 and the deal was announced on July 12. Film columnists across the country announced the news and a story in the *Los Angeles Times* heralded Hitchcock as Selznick's "prize acquisition."

Hitchcock would depart for England on July 13 and news of America's gain was seen as a huge loss for the British film industry and England as a whole. Hitchcock intended to leave England in January 1939 after completing his next film, *Jamaica Inn*.

As first, plans were that Hitchcock would begin exploratory work on *Titanic* as early as August, but Selznick decided to postpone the project for unknown reasons. When Hitchcock pushed him for a reason, Selznick only told Hitchcock to not relay the news to the media not wanting to, "give the impression that we have relaxed plans for *Titanic* lest someone else be encouraged to go ahead with it."

While Selznick now considered several options for the first Hitchcock picture, *Rebecca* was touted to be the director's second film for Selznick International. One idea mentioned was a film version of the London play, "The Flashing Stream" with Carole Lombard as its star.

In the fall, *Variety* was still touting *Titanic* as Hitchcock's first Hollywood feature and Hitchcock continued with plans for the film, going so far as to meet with London's Board of Trade on November 2 to ease their concerns that Hitchcock's direction of the tragic demise of so many innocent passengers would scare off ocean travelers. "They seem to think that if I recapture all the horror and violence of the situation it will stop people from going on cruises," complained Hitchcock. The director persuaded them that his film would depict the heroism of the day and promoted the advancements in British seamanship and current life-saving measures of the day.

Film Weekly reported in early 1939 that *Titanic* and *Rebecca* would be the director's first two pictures in Hollywood. "Working under new conditions with an entirely fresh crowd of people will be like a tonic. I am itching to get my hands on some of those American stars," Hitchcock told the press.

As the months wore on *Titanic* began to fade as a likely Hitchcock film when Selznick decided *Rebecca* would be the director's first Hollywood movie. By Mid-November Hitchcock finally got word that *Titanic* was history and *Rebecca* was to be the focus of his attention. However, Selznick was unwilling to provide Hitchcock a January or February 1939 start date for his film because of other pending business. Hitchcock was furious, not only that he had wasted time on the elusive *Titanic* picture, but he would suffer several months of doing nothing, with the time too short to work on any other films.

Hitchcock did get a big boost when he was named "Best Director of 1938" by the New York Film Critics. Not wanting the director to accept a film on loan for another studio as was permitted under his current deal, Selznick renegotiated Hitchcock's original contract preventing him from accepting another picture by offering him a substantial salary increase for the Selznick International Pictures he would direct. Hitchcock gladly accepted the added pay and set sights on moving to the United States, setting sail on March 4, 1939.

Rebecca would ultimately succeed as Hitchcock's first Hollywood picture. Arriving in theaters in 1940 at a cost of just under $1.3 million, and starring Laurence Olivier and Joan Fontaine, the film would gross $6 million and earn Selznick an Academy Award as Producer of the Year. Hitchcock would lose the elusive Best Director Oscar to John Ford for *The Grapes of Wrath*.

Titanic would eventually make its American movie debut in 1953 when Jean Negulesco directed Clifton Webb and Barbara Stanwyck in a Twentieth-Century Fox telling of the tale. Released on April 16, 1953, 39 years after the sinking of the ocean liner, the $1.8 million film would earn more than $2.2 million at the box office.

Hitchcock's closest filmmaking connection to *Titanic* would come in 1944 when his film *Lifeboat* was released. The film would earn him an Academy Award nomination for Best Director and centered on a small band of survivors aboard a lifeboat after the sinking of their ocean liner.

four

THE LOST HITCHCOCKS

"The public must be rooting for the character; they should almost be helping him to achieve his goal."

- Alfred Hitchcock

Remaking 'The Lodger'

The novel *The Lodger*, by Marie Belloc Lowndes, was adapted into play called *Who Is He?*, as a fictionalized re-telling of the story of London's Jack The Ripper murders. Alfred Hitchcock saw the stage version of the play in 1915 and liked the idea enough to think the story held promise as a feature film. "The action was set in a house that took in roomers and the landlady wondered whether her new boarder was Jack the Ripper or not," Hitchcock recalled.

Hitchcock recalled the play a number of years later and dusted off the novel version, thinking the concept would be perfect as his next film. In 1927, *The Lodger* would become Hitchcock's third credited feature film as a director. The British silent film starred Marie Ault, Arthur Chesney, June Tripp, Malcolm Keen, and Ivor Novello. Released in February 1927, the film begins dramatically with the face of a screaming young blond woman who becomes the seventh victim of a serial killer referred to as "The Avenger." He targets young blond women on Tuesday evenings. "I treated it very simply, purely from her [the landlady's] point of view," said Hitchcock.

The film was significant to Hitchcock for several reasons. First, it was his first thriller. While not yet known as the master of suspense, the genre would later become synonymous with the director and many of its elements would be featured in Hitchcock's future films.

In *The Lodger,* the title character is portrayed by Ivor Novello. He is a man who is unjustly accused of being a serial killer by a jealous detective, another common theme for the director. The film would also

mark Hitchcock's first cameo appearance, something fans would later come to expect in his movies.

For the climax of the silent version, Hitchcock wanted an ambiguous ending, leaving his audience wondering if *The Lodger* could possibly be the killer after all, but the studio didn't want there to be any chance that viewers might come away believing that the star might actually be a murderer. The studio executives rejected Hitchcock's plans, forcing the director to film it leaving no doubt about the identity of the killer. With Hitchcock only on his third film as a director, he wasn't in a position to argue, so he followed his orders, but knew his way was better. "They wouldn't let Novello even be considered as a villain," recalled Hitchcock. "The publicity angle carried the day, and we had to change the script to show that without a doubt he was innocent. So I just never even showed the real murderer."

Because *The Lodger* was intended to end with ambiguity as to whether or not the lodger is innocent, and Hitch hoped that if he got a second chance to film the story he would be more successful in telling his version of the tale. Back in 1926, when Ivor Novello was cast in the role, the studio demanded alterations to the script because they didn't want Novello to be even suspected as a villain.

Hitchcock compromised by avoiding to show the true killer onscreen. However, when producer Michael Balcon saw Hitchcock's completed film he was furious at the way Hitchcock got around the issue. The studio nearly cancelled the release *The Lodger*. In the end, the studio opted to not waste the money spent on the footage film and decided to alter some of the title cards and reshoot a few minor scenes.

Even without the ending he desired, *The Lodger* was a hit and film historians see the film's importance as a defining mark in his career as a filmmaker. Through suspense films, "Hitchcock found his voice," said the historians. The success of the film and the style, direction and themes would become key elements through the remainder of his career. While not his first film, Hitchcock told Francois Truffaut, "*The Lodger* was the first true Hitchcock movie."

THE LOST HITCHCOCKS

After leaving the United Kingdom for America in the 1930, and settling into Hollywood, Hitchcock would go onto much bigger and better pictures. The financing was bigger, the stars were brighter, the sets, scripts, and crews were stronger, and the acclaim greater. After his first Oscar nomination for *Rebecca* for Best Director and the Academy Award for Best Picture for the same film, Hitchcock would begin to earn more control over the movies he would make and the ways his stories were told. He never wanted to repeat the experience of *The Lodger* and have to

Ivor Novello was one of the stars of 'The Lodger' in 1927.

succumb to the demands of studio executives.

Hitchcock longed to remake the film, telling Truffaut, years later, that of all his films, *The Lodger* was the one he most desired to remake. "... An excellent story filmed without sound, which was the basis for two later versions by other directors."

In the 1940s Hitchcock intended to buy the film rights to the novel, hoping to remake *The Lodger,* but this time more closely to the one he originally had intended to film. In addition, through the use of sound, and color, Hitchcock thought he'd be able to do something remarkable with the story, outdoing himself. With a colorized version of the film, Hitchcock saw an opportunity to shed new light on his story. "Color for reason, not just color to knock people's eyes out." he once said. "Make color an actor, a defined part of the whole. Make it work as an actor instead of scenery."

For *The Lodger*, Hitchcock saw "natural color used naturally." He felt that with color he might add a new aspect to foggy London. "I want to show how street lamps seem to drop deeper yellow tears into that swirling mess of vaporous sulfur."

He spoke of filming the interiors with drab settings, but splashes of color. "A London family in a dismal basement dining room, all browns and grays and blacks," he described. "When suddenly the plaster in the ceiling gets first damp, then pink, then red, and a drop of red falls down and splashes onto a while tablecloth and spreads out as another drop joins it. When we rush upstairs, expecting the worst, we find a man has upset a bottle of red ink and it is dripping through his floor and the ceiling below."

However, not all the color would be benign. "I can even see a closeup of two murderous eyes, the white of the eyeballs stained by crimson red veins ... inflamed eyes. Not makeup, actually inflamed eyes."

However, Hitchcock was unable to convince a major studio to back the idea, and financially he was not yet in a position to go it alone. "Very often the story line is jeopardized because a star cannot be a villain," said the director.

After his release of *The Lodger*, other films telling the same tale have resulted, but never from the master of suspense. "Since then there have been two or three remakes, but they are too elaborate," Hitch told Truffaut.

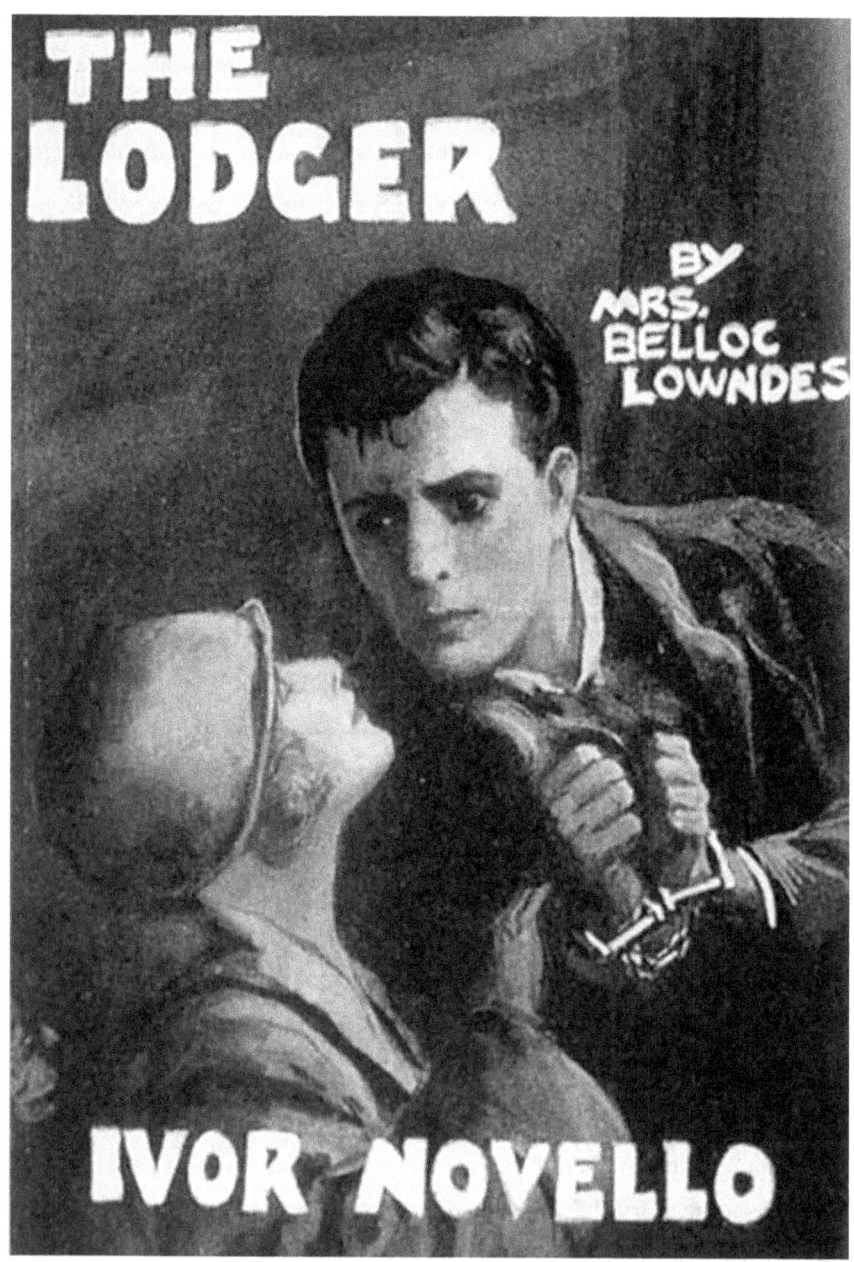

THE LOST HITCHCOCKS

Had Hitchcock been given the green light to remake *The Lodger*, dialog and sound would have added a new layer to his storytelling, allowing sound to bring new suspense and help move the story forward. His man unjustly accused, would remain intact. Hitchcock never reached the stage of casting, so no leading man was ever mentioned. Yet, knowing Hitchcock, he would want to leave viewers guessing about the identity of the true killer. "In a story of this kind, I might have liked him to go off in the night, so that we would never know for sure," said Hitch.

Another major stumbling block for the director was that Mrs. Belloc Lowndes, author of the novel, hated the silent version and refused to sell the rights to Hitchcock. Even after Hitchcock explained that problems with the original were not his fault and he intended to correct the errors from the earlier version, the $20,000 price tag was too steep for the director.

Hitchcock explained to Francois Truffaut, years later, that a large portion of the film, especially the early scenes leading up to the introduction of the lead character, would have been changed. " Naturally, many of these visual devices would be superfluous today because we would use sound effects. The sound of the steps and so on."

The selection of his star would have again been difficult, but key to the story. It would have been unlikely for a major studio to allow a leading man like Gregory Peck or Cary Grant to be an implied serial killer. Though, Hitchcock would dabble with that scenario years later with both those leading men, with Cary Grant in *Suspicion*, and Gregory Peck in *Spellbound*, when both were positioned as possible killers. However, Hitchcock never got his way again with both men being clearly innocent by the end of the movie.

An interesting footnote is that Hitchcock did eventually secure the rights to *The Lodger* in the early 1940s to retell the story. However, film was not the channel he would use. Hitchcock had long been a fan of evening radio programs and toyed with the idea of producing a regular program of his own to promote himself and his work.

United Artists and Walter Wanger expressed interest in the idea of a nightime Hitchcock radio program, and David O. Selznick also thought the idea had potential. Hitchcock suggested using his rights to *The Lodger* as a way to broadcast a retelling of the tale.

Making use of two of his stars from *Foreign Correspondent*, Hitchcock got Herbert Marshall and Edmund Gwynne to perform in the show. Gwynne, in fact, had helped put up some of the funding for the rights to the story. Broadcast on July 22, 1940, as part of the *Forecast* series, this version stayed true to the novel and left open the question as to whether the key character was or was not the killer stalking London. Viewers were encouraged to write in their throughts one whether *The Lodger* was or was not a serial killer, and they were also asked to request a regular Hitchcock series. However, David O. Selznick refused to consider Hitchcock taking part in a regular radio program and a Hitchcock show would never be heard.

Notably, it was during this brief flirtation with radio that a New York advertising man came up with the idea of calling Hitchcock the "Master of Suspense." While the radio program never materialized, the catchy phrase became Hitchcock's moniker.

five

THE LOST HITCHCOCKS

"A major problem with this sort of film is getting an actor of stature to play the central figure. I've learned from experience that whenever the hero isn't portrayed by a star, the whole picture suffers, you see, because audiences are far less concerned about the predicament of a character who's played by someone they don't know."

- Alfred Hitchcock

Greenmantle

The 39 Steps was Hitchcock's 1935 British thriller with Robert Donat and Madeleine Carroll. Loosely based on a 1915 adventure novel called *The Thirty-Nine Steps* by John Buchan, the film takes place in London, focusing on an ordinary man caught up in extraordinary circumstances. Richard Hannay is enlisted into helping a counter-espionage agent stop a group of spies called "The 39 Steps" who are attempting to get their hands on top-secret information. After the agent is killed, Hannay is accused of his murder and has to stop the spies, as well as prove his innocence.

Gaumont-British, the producer of *The 39 Steps,* saw the thriller's potential by branching out into international markets, like the United States, and the resulting success of the movie helped put Hitchcock on the map.

In 1916, John Buchan returned with his second novel. *Greenmantle* would actually be the second of five novels featuring the character of Richard Hannay. Published in 1916 by Hodder & Stoughton in London, *Greenmantle* was one of two Hannay novels set during the First World War. The other, *Mr. Standfast,* was published in 1919. *The Thirty-Nine Steps,* on the other hand, takes place immediately preceding the war.

The story begins in November 1915, as Hannay and a friend, who he assisted in *The Thirty-Nine Steps,* are once again called into duty. A political situation in the Middle East suggests that German and Turkish criminals are plotting to cause trouble, intent on creating turmoil in Middle East, India, and North Africa. Hannay is asked to investigate. He accepts the dangerous assignment, which takes him across Europe, Africa, and the Middle East.

Greenmantle is another fictional story, loosely based on the character and exploits of T. E. Lawrence, the real-life title character from *Lawrence of Arabia.* Richard Hannay, the main character in *The 39 Steps,* takes on the Lawrence role. Hitchcock enjoyed the novel and began looking to make a film version after the success of *The 39 Steps* in 1935. By 1939, after arriving in Hollywood, Hitchcock hoped to gain financing to do a major studio version and thought Cary Grant would be ideal the role of Hannay, with Ingrid Bergman as his co-star. Hitch wanted to up the ante with major stars and not return with Donat and Carroll from *The 39 Steps*. One person Hitch thought he might get to help him bankroll the film was producer Walter Wanger.

Walter Wanger was an American film producer whose work often carried social messages, mixed with romance and drama. His melodramas were influenced by European films, in part from his experience in Europe during World War I. His movie career began in 1920 at Paramount Pictures, but by 1921, unhappy at Paramount, he left the studio,

deciding instead to travel to Britain to work as a theatre manager. During his time in London, he met and became friends with Hitchcock.

Wagner's serious and message-driven material often needed serious directors. Working with the likes of Fritz Lange, Rouben Mamoulian, and Frank Capra, Wanger knew good directors were key to getting the message through even when it was wrapped in an entertaining and engaging drama. Hitchcock intrigued Wagner and he longed to work with him.

By the late 1930s he was releasing films through United Artists and Wanger knew Hitchcock was looking to move to Hollywood and was being courted by David O. Selznick. Wanger wanted to strike a deal with Hitchcock, but he couldn't compete with Selznick's offer.

In 1935, Wanger purchased the rights to Vincent Sheean's journalist memoir, *Personal History*, and after several failed adaptations he finally came up with a usable script in 1940. With Hitchcock now making films in the United States under contract to David O. Selznick, Wanger approached him to see if he was available to direct the film. On loan, Hitchcock dove into *Personal History*, which eventually transitioned into the film *Foreign Correspondent*. Free from the pressure and scrutiny of Selznick, the production started in March 1940 and wrapped up quickly, ending in early June. After filming, Hitchcock headed home to England for a brief holiday, returning in July, when he and Wanger began discussing the idea of another film together. Wanger was at the end of his distribution deal with United Artists and Hitchcock was looking for his next project. *Greenmantle* came forth as the most likely candidate.

Hitchcock proposed the idea of a follow up to *The 39 Steps*, and Wanger found the idea had strong potential, but if they were to go it without a major studio, stars like Cary Grant and Ingrid Bergman wouldn't be an option. Hitchcock contacted Robert Donat, star of the original film, about bringing him over to the United States to make the Hollywood sequel. Donat was reluctant to leave England, but Hitchcock was initially not deterred. If Donat was a no-show, he had other possible actors who could fill the part.

THE LOST HITCHCOCKS

Things got difficult when Selznick refused to loan Hitchcock out to Wanger for another production. Offers for Hitchcock's services arrived regularly to David O. Selznick and he found he could pit the offers against each other to raise the asking price, making top dollar for Hitchcock's directing responsibilities. In fact, Hitchcock was more valuable to Selznick on loan than he was as his director. Wagner would only gain Hitchcock's services if he could offer more than anyone else for his services, even if Hitchcock wanted to work with him.

Warner Bros. expressed interest in signing a deal with Wanger. The studio was strongly in favor of getting several Hitchcock pictures and Hal Wallis, head of production at Warner Bros., was eager to make a deal. Wanger then began working on negotiating for the screen rights to *Greenmantle* shortly after. In February 1940, however, the deal hit a roadblock when author of the novel, John Buchan, suffered a severe head injury from a fall, after a stroke. After two surgeries to repair the damage, Buchan died on February 11. Because his estate held the rights to his work, the lawyers wanted a hefty sum for film rights to *Greenmantle,* putting it out of reach for Wanger.

The cost of the film rights, coupled with the budget estimates to film *Greenmantle* caused Warner Bros. to back out. Wanger took the production idea to Twentieth-Century Fox where Darryl Zanuck expressed interest in the film. However, he too would ultimately back out after seeing the cost estimates to film the movie. As much as the studios wanted to have Hitchcock on their lot, the price tag for *Greenmantle* was simply too steep.

Over at MGM, studio executives also expressed interest in a Hitchcock picture and approached the director about making a film about a female criminal with a dark past and a gruesome scar on her face. She undergoes cosmetic surgery to remove the scar in hopes of changing her life for the better. Titled *A Woman's Face*, Hitchcock had mixed feelings about making the film with its intended star, Joan Crawford. MGM, however, promised to consider *Greenmantle* as a second feature to follow on the heels of a successful film completion of *A Woman's Face*. Hitchcock considered the deal.

However, the MGM deal again soured over the fees and the demands David O. Selznick was making for his star director. Hitchcock was then courted by RKO to direct the film version of Francis Iles' novel, *Before the Fact*. Hitchcock immediately expressed interest, as he was well aware of Iles' work and had hoped one day he might direct a film version of one of his crime stories. Hitchcock again suggested the idea of *Greenmantle* as a follow-up feature, but RKO wasn't particularly interested in an expensive production of *Greenmantle*.

Meanwhile, over at Columbia, a screenplay called *And Now Goodbye* was being finalized for production when the studio inquired to Selznick about having Hitchcock direct its film. Hitchcock, again, was willing to consider the project, but wanted a two-picture deal with *Greenmantle* as the follow up feature. Columbia was open to the idea, but it still had to be the studio that would make the best offer to Selznick to secure the director's services.

Selznick rejected the offers from Warner Bros., Twentieth-Century Fox, MGM and Columbia, selecting RKO as the studio Hitchcock would work for next. Unfortunately for Hitchcock and Wanger, RKO had no interest in making *Greenmantle*. While the deal was for two films, Hitchcock would direct *Mr. and Mrs. Smith* as the first film. Then, instead of *Greenmantle, Before the Fact* would be the follow up feature, but by the time it hit the big screen the film would be retitled *Suspicion*.

six

THE LOST HITCHCOCKS

"I'd bought a story called 'Flamingo Feather,' written by a South African author who was also a diplomat. His name was Laurens van der Post. It was the story of mysterious happenings in South Africa today."

— **Alfred Hitchcock**

Flamingo Feather

Hitchcock engaged in a lifelong love of travel, and during his most productive years, he would look for ways to mix business with pleasure by making his movies in exotic locations, allowing him multiple opportunities to visit locales for location scouting before a film and location shooting during production. Films like *To Catch a Thief, The Man Who Knew Too Much, Stage Fright, I Confess, Vertigo, The Birds* and *Frenzy* allowed him to vacation in places he loved while expensing them as part of a picture.

From 1949 through 1956 his travels would take him around the globe, from New York and Washington DC, to Quebec, London, Morocco, Africa, The French Riviera, and his personal favorite, Saint Moritz. When it wasn't for work on a film itself, Hitch used travel as a public relations opportunity as well. He would travel the world promoting his

films, making specific junkets to Japan, Indonesia, Australia and Europe to publicize his pictures, meeting with the press and conducting interviews for international publications to talk about himself and his work. Extending the trips to include lengthy vacations for himself and his wife, and sometimes other family and friends, was often a part of the plan.

Even films he wouldn't complete would give him the chance to travel for a potential film. After dropping a project, he could still write off much of the expense. *Flamingo Feather*, for Paramount Pictures, would be just such a project.

Founder of Paramount Pictures, Adolph Zukor, was an early investor in nickelodeons, believing the short movies appealed to the working-class as an affordable escape from ordinary life. With partners Daniel Frohman and Charles Frohman he saw feature-length films as appealing to the middle class as well, and the trio went into business in 1912, first as the Famous Players Film Company.

By mid-1913, Famous Players had five films completed, and Zukor was on his way to success, while aspiring producer Jesse L. Lasky launched Lasky Feature Play Company, and both Lasky and Famous Players released their films through a start-up company, Paramount Pictures Corporation, formed, also in 1913, by Utah theatre owner W. W. Hodkinson.

Paramount was the first successful nationwide distributor and in 1916, Zukor spearheaded a merger of his Famous Players, the Lasky Company, and Paramount. Paramount Pictures would quickly become one of the dominant players in modern day motion pictures.

By the 1950s, the studio, like all other major studios, was angling for top rate directors to provide movies that would generate big box office and critical acclaim while competing with the new medium of television. Hitchcock, being one of the most prolific and popular directors working, was being courted and used by all the major studios.

Hitchcock's association with Paramount, aside from his early career work in London, began as a single film deal when he was on loan to the studio by Warner Bros. for *Rear Window*. Because star Jimmy

Stewart had a multi-picture deal with Paramount, Warner Bros. agreed to loan the director out in exchange for sharing film distribution rights in 1954. The one-picture deal quickly evolved into a lucrative contract for nine films for the studio, five directed and produced by Hitchcock, and an additional four produced by the studio with only direction by the master of suspense. In addition to a bump in salary for directing duties, Hitch also earned a cut of the profits from the films and was given more creative control to make only films he envisioned.

One of the films Hitchcock made under the Paramount deal was a reworking of his 1934 British film, *The Man Who Knew Too Much*. Starring Jimmy Stewart and Doris Day, the production took cast and crew to Africa in the spring and summer of 1955.

Working largely in Marrakech, Hitchcock was able to get the authentic look he was after, although he and his stars had to struggle with "ungodly hot" weather and constant reminders of the poverty and poor living conditions of many of its people. Even so, Hitch managed to treat himself and his production team to the best restaurants and accommodations during their African stay.

In June 1955, while covering his latest project, *Variety* reported news of Hitchcock's intentions to make a follow up film in Africa called *Flamingo Feather*. "Alfred Hitchcock has a pair of films coming up which will be filmed in Africa. The director and stars James Stewart and Doris Day recently returned to London from Marrakech, French Morocco, where filming on *The Man Who Knew Too Much* started on May 12."

While the media reported prolifically on his current project, little had been reported on his plans for another film set in Africa until *Variety* broke the news. "On Hitch's future slate is "Flamingo Feather," based on Laurens van der Post, and dealing with a contemporary adventure set in Africa. The director and Stewart plan a safari to film the property."

Paramount had actually optioned the rights to the 1955 novel *Flamingo Feather* by Laurens van der Post with plans for the film adaptation by Hitchcock. Hitchcock was attracted to the mystery and suspense angles of the book. "It was the story of mysterious happenings in

South Africa today. A lot of people were involved; it was hinged around a secret compound in which large numbers of natives were being trained under Russian command."

It would be one of the four films produced by the studio and directed by Hitch. The director was juggling multiple projects at the time. In addition to films already in production like *To Catch a Thief*, *The Man Who Knew Too Much*, and *The Trouble With Harry*, another idea tentatively titled "The Man in Lincoln's Nose," which would ultimately become *North by Northwest*, was in development. Paramount had also commissioned a synopsis of *D'Entre les Mortes* ("From Among the Dead") in 1954, before it was even translated into English, because Hitch thought the idea had potential for a film. Hitchcock was not sure what order his series of projects would fall, but he was flush with film prospects for the remainder of the decade.

While work began on the adaptation of *Flamingo Feather*, another endeavor drew Hitchcock's attention – television. In 1955, CBS offered Hitchcock $125,000 per episode for a suspense series called *Alfred Hitchcock Presents*. While the director would supervise the series, he would actually only direct a handful of episodes and film brief studio introductions and endings for each show.

If this mountain of work wasn't enough to keep the prolific director busy, he also had a film due for Warner Bros. called *The Wrong Man*, that would require him to step away from Paramount for a period in order to complete the film.

Following the completion of *The Man Who Knew Too Much* and *The Wrong Man*, Hitchcock's plan was to film *Flamingo Feather*, which the press described as, "an anti-communist tale in the guise of a Buchanesque adventure story."

Angus MacPhail, who had provided some of the substance behind *The Man Who Knew Too Much*, was approached to draft the screenplay for *Flamingo Feather*, while John Michael Hayes would be hired to polish the dialogue and complete the final script. Hitch had worked with Hayes on *Rear Window*.

Jimmy Stewart enjoyed his experience in Africa for *The Man Who Knew Too Much*, so much so, that he expressed interest in starring in *Flamingo Feather* and Hitchcock initially hoped to draw Grace Kelly back to Hollywood from Monaco, but it was a long shot.

Jimmy Stewart was the intended star of 'Flamingo Feather.'

Hitchcock finished the production phase of *The Wrong Man* in June 1956 and turned his attention to scouting locations for *Flamingo Feather*. Alfred and Alma, along with Herbert Coleman and Doc Erickson, embarked on a "research trip" for the film at the end of May 1956. After receiving shots to prevent yellow fever, the Hitchcocks left New York, aboard the RMS Queen Elizabeth. They headed to England where they were met by Coleman and Erickson, who had both flown in from the states.

After a week in London, meeting with officials at the Colonial Office and visiting the novel's author, Laurens van der Post, at his home near London to discuss the story's translation to film, they set forth on their next leg of their journey. After stops in Madrid and Rome, Hitchcock departed for Johannesburg, South Africa. From there, stops in Swaziland, Pretoria, and Durban would occur.

While Hitchcock was in Madrid, Coleman and Erickson headed to Cannes, "to renew friendships with the French film workers who'd helped us make *To Catch a Thief*," recalled Coleman. They reconnected in Rome. In Italy, Hitchcock planned to meet with Cary Grant who he hoped to get to star in the film, rather than Stewart. At the airport, a collection of Italian press was waiting when Hitchcock arrived. Assuming they were there for him, he was disappointed to learn they were actually waiting for French boxer Robert Cohen to arrive on a later flight, but photographers grabbed some shots of Hitchcock nonetheless.

Alfred and Alma left Rome for South Africa, arriving in Johannesburg at the end of June. Location scouting never really took place once Hitchcock arrived in South Africa. Some say he had actually begun to lose interest in the concept before he even got there and the trip was more of a vacation than work. Using the film idea as a reason for the trip allowed the bill for a holiday to be disguised as work.

Flamingo Feather became doomed due to logistical pitfalls. The inability to lure Grace Kelly out of retirement after her April 1956 wedding to Prince Rainier of Monaco was the first blow. Then Cary Grant's lack of interest caused Hitch to lose interest in the project, even though he still had Jimmy Stewart as a back up. Paramount raised concerns about the politics of the story, though Hitchcock felt that could be managed in much the same way he downplayed politics in *The Man Who Knew Too Much*. The biggest pitfall of the film came in the form of the budget. The studio and the scouting team quickly realized it would be quite expensive to film in Africa. According to Coleman, the group had decided, "it was simply too impracticable to film in Africa."

Hitchcock had also learned in Africa that he would have limited access to available actors and extras, as well as major challenges for camera and sound equipment for the location filming. "I went to South Africa to do some advance research on the shooting, and I found out that there was no chance of getting fifty thousand Africans we needed."

Hitchcock recalled that when asked why he couldn't get the large number of Afircans he needed, he was told, "the natives work on the pineapple plantations and at many other jobs and the work couldn't be stopped for a movie."

Ultimately, the director would have had to resort to using soundstages in Hollywood for more of the film than planned. Hitchcock even toured the Valley of a Thousand Hills in Natal, a picturesque spot on the edge of densely covered hills outside Durban where Zulu people lived in traditional homesteads. Hitchcock determined that the hills and valleys could more easily be replicated outside Hollywood than to pay a costly sum to film on location. "We can get the same scenery sixty miles north of Los Angeles," Hitch commented.

Once Hitchcock became convinced it would be impossible to film there, his location-scouting trip turned into a vacation with visits to Livingstone, Southern Rhodesia, Victoria Falls, Nairobi, and Kenya. Hitchcock had relatives in the area and managed a visit with his aunt, Emma Mary Rhodes, before returning to London.

In London, Hitchcock regrouped and began to think about how to proceed. Dropping *Flamingo Feather* seemed the only sensible thing to do and Hitch thought another project, an American version of *D'Entre les Mortes,* might be best suited to take its place. Hitchcock's sister Nellie joined him and Alma during their return voyage aboard the Queen Elizabeth to America as the director mulled over the order of his films and the final fate of *Flamingo Feather*.

During the voyage, they learned of the collision between the SS Andrea Doria and the MS Stockholm off the coast of Nantucket, Massachusetts. The tragedy cast a cloud over their return journey when they learned 46 people had lost their lives. Among the survivors from the Andrea Doria was actress Ruth Roman, who had worked for Hitchcock on *Strangers on a Train*. Cary Grant's wife Betsy Drake was also rescued from the ship.

By the time Hitchcock returned to Hollywood, he had abandoned *Flamingo Feather* in favor of his *D'Entre les Mortes* concept. The film would ultimately become *Vertigo*.

THE LOST HITCHCOCKS

seven

THE LOST HITCHCOCKS

"Naturally, I expect to go forward, to advance with each new picture, but to what degree I will succeed, I don't know."

- Alfred Hitchcock

Hamlet

St. Ignatius College was founded by Jesuit Fathers in 1894 as a day school for young men. Located in Stamford Hill, an 11-year-old Alfred Hitchcock began attending the school in October 1910. Traveling by train each day, the young Alfred first attended mass before heading to classes. The school consisted of an elementary school, a college, a church and a chapel, and had some 250 students in attendance around the time of Hitchcock's enrollment.

One of the things instilled in Hitchcock during his school days at St. Ignatius were the writings of William Shakespeare. Along with the works of Longfellow, Dante, Dickens and Defoe, the writings of Shakespeare were committed to memory and performed aloud in their entirety as part of the curriculum.

Hitchcock loved Shakespeare, and as a filmmaker he occasionally found himself incorporating elements of his storytelling into his movies. Both *Rich and Strange* and *The Man Who Knew Too Much* bor-

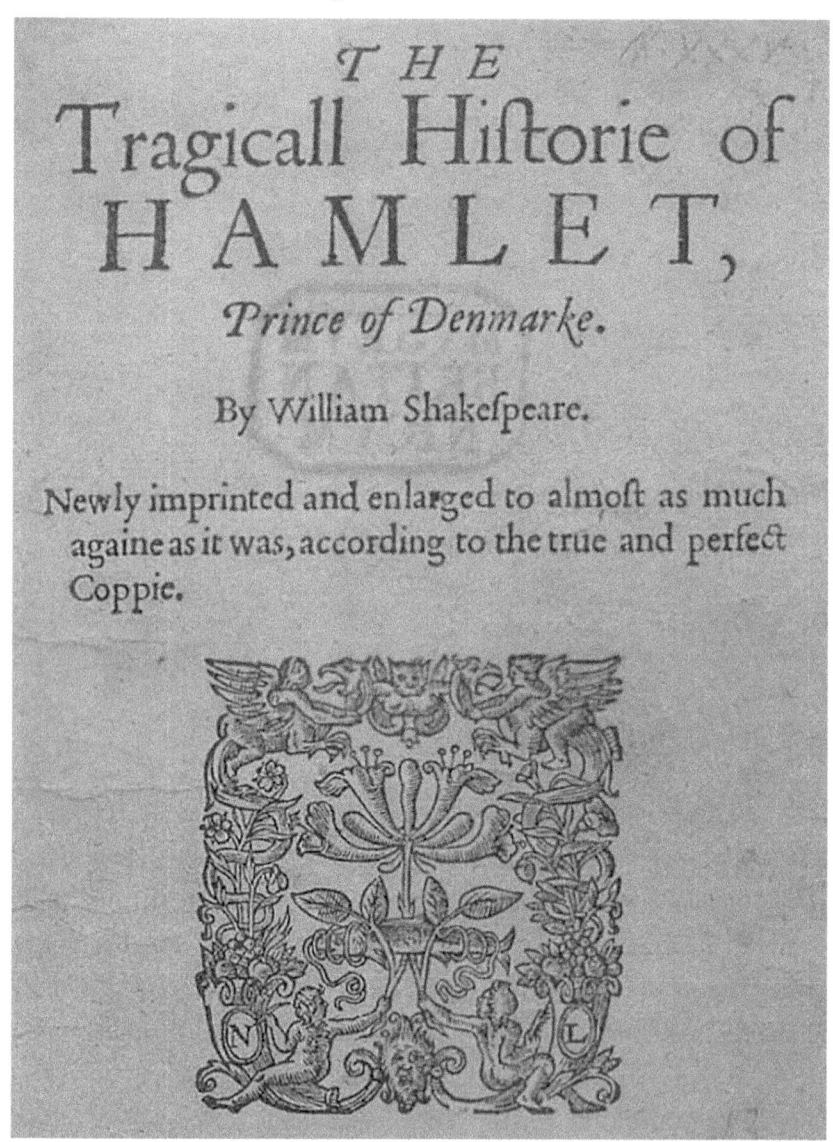

rowed snippets of his work and Hitchcock's fascination with mother-son relationships and father-daughter pairings can also be traced back to his readings as a boy.

In 1946, Hitchcock had several films in development, including *Under Capricorn* and *The Paradine Case*, but was also in the process of forming his own production company with Sidney Bernstein, a British media aristocrat and lifelong friend of Hitchcock's, dating back to the 1920s. Bernstein was looking for a post-war career and Hitchcock proposed the production studio as something they could do together.

Forming Transatlantic Pictures in the summer of 1945, the duo hoped to use the production house to make independent films without oversight from powerful studio executives looking to control them and their films. Transatlantic would hopefully reap the rewards of box office success by doing movies Hitchcock's way, with him in control of the concepts behind each film.

At one point Hitchcock pitched the idea of the production company to Cary Grant as well, but Grant was reluctant to join the fledgling company, though he was willing to consider starring in some of its films.

The first idea they discussed was a project called "Weep No More" a suspense drama that was intended for RKO. Over a series of long lunches at a Mexican restaurant just across the street from RKO, Hitchcock and Grant tried for weeks to build out the idea for the movie. A basic plot had barely formed, with Hitchcock focusing his time on building out the characters, hoping to keep Grant interested in the project.

As the weeks went by, Grant began to lose interest in the idea and "Weep No More" failed to develop into a cohesive story, let alone a script. Hitch knew Grant's interest was waning, but wanted to keep him lined up as the star of one of his upcoming features. One afternoon, while Grant was filming *None but the Lonely Heart* at Warner Bros., Hitch visited him on the set to pitch him an idea of another film that could be crafted to showcase him at his best. Hitchcock's idea was a modern day *Hamlet*. The plan was to transform Shakespeare's text into modern English and to try and present the *Hamlet* story as a "psychological melodrama," and with Cary Grant in the lead role.

Cary Grant reportedly gave the concept a "tentative endorsement," and that was all Hitchcock needed. He quickly added *Hamlet* to

Cary Grant was the intended star of Hitchcock's 'Hamlet.'

his roster of upcoming films for his fledgling Transatlantic Pictures with Grant penciled in as its star. The nice thing about using *Hamlet* was that it would be cheap to make since Shakespeare's work was part of the public domain and the director didn't have to negotiate rights to his work.

For Cary Grant it would have marked a turning point in his career as he edged away from heroic casting into darker and more complex characters. *Hamlet* might have appealed to him, in part, because of the deep and complex relationship between the main character and his mother. Grant had his own challenges in that department.

Born in England as Archibald Alexander Leach, his mother was diagnosed with clinical depression after the death of a child. She was placed in a mental institution when he was just nine years old. First he was told she had gone on a long holiday, but later informed that she had died. As a young boy, Grant struggled to cope with the loss of his mother. He continued to believe she had died until the age of 31 when he learned she was, in fact, very much alive. His father admitted to him that he had been lying to him for years. Shortly before his death, Grant's father confessed, adding that he could find her alive in a psychiatric facility where he was able to reestablish a relationship with his mother.

Grant's career began with the Bob Pender Stage Troupe, around 1919, when he began performing as a stilt walker. In 1920 the group traveled to the United States aboard RMS Olympic, for a two-year tour of the country. By they time the troupe was ready to return, Cary decided to remain in the U.S. and find work on the stage. He spent time working the vaudeville circuit where his experience as a stilt walker, acrobat, juggler, and mime were put to good use. In 1942 he became a U.S. citizen and legally changed his name from Archibald Leach to Cary Grant.

Cary arrived in Hollywood in 1931 and soon found his way into the movies with his good looks and talent. He appeared as a leading man opposite Marlene Dietrich in *Blonde Venus* in 1932, and then opposite Mae West in *She Done Him Wrong* and *I'm No Angel*, both released 1933.

In 1936 he signed with Columbia Pictures and was loaned out for

MGM's *Topper*, which became a big hit in 1937. *The Awful Truth*, also in 1937, showed how deft he could be at light comedy and was followed by *The Philadelphia Story* in 1940.

He then starred in a handful of screwball comedies, including *His Girl Friday* and *My Favorite Wife,* both in 1940. *Suspicion*, in 1941, would mark the start of his relationship with Alfred Hitchcock, as the first of four films with the director and a chance to play much more complex characters.

In 1945, Hitchcock proposed the idea of a modernized version of *Hamlet* that would be set in England. Cary would once again be able to stretch himself in a psychological melodrama and Hitchcock cabled his new partner Sidney Bernstein with the idea. Dan O'Shea, a vice president for Selznick International Pictures, reportedly agreed that the idea held promise.

In the telegram to Bernstein, Hitchcock wrote, "Would like to get your reaction to the following idea for our English production; This idea would illustrate itself clearer to you if I indicated the billing which would be, "Sidney Bernstein presents Cary Grant as Alfred Hitchcock's *Hamlet*, a modern thriller by William Shakespeare."

Hitchcock's telegram then fleshed out the idea further with, "As you will see the idea is to take the Shakespeare text and transcribe it into modern English. The play would have an English setting and would be presented as a psychological melodrama. I was over to see Cary Grant yesterday at Warner's studio and he expressed great enthusiasm for the idea. I told Dan O'Shea about it and his reaction was that it would be a terrific piece of showmanship. The most essential thing would be to make certain that the public realized that they would be seeing a modern story. The process required to get a script of this would be as follows. First of all to get a professor of English to take the original play and do a modern language version of it, then to turn this into a film treatment and to reinterpret the situations into modern idiom. After this process has been completed the next step would be to take this treatment with its straightforward English dialogue and have it gone over by a top playwright for the final version. Naturally, I am concerned about maintaining secrecy on this because the idea is in public domain and could easily be stolen if word leaked out because it is a very hard thing to register."

The director then posed additional questions to Bernstein, asking, "Do you think a simultaneous announcement both here and in London would be the best means of safe guarding the property assuming you like the idea? Do you think it possible for you to find somebody to do the first dialogue transcript in dialogue form, preferably a professor of English - but definitely no one in show business? After this is completed then I would like to have some stooge writer cut here, such as Jock Orton, who would be inexpensive, but who would carry out my idea for the pictorial, and incremental treatment of the action. I think he could be

Laurence Olivier would ultimately star in Hollywood's 'Hamlet.'

gotten for around $500 a week with a six-month's guarantee. The final phase we could discuss together when you get out here. Please telephone me if you need any clarification. Love Hitch."

When word leaked out to the press that Hitchcock and Bernstein had not only formed their production company, *Under Capricorn* was slated as their first film, and it would be followed by Cary Grant in *Hamlet*.

In September 1945 the *Aberdeen Journal* in England reported the news that, "Mr. Alfred Hitchcock, the British film director who has been working in Hollywood for some years, is returning to this country this week. During his stay lasting some months he will begin a modernized version of 'Hamlet.'"

The newspaper was even aware of the film's impending star, writing, "In collaboration with Cary Grant, the Bristol-born film star, Mr. Hitchcock has just formed a new and independent company, and their first joint venture will be this ambitious production of Shakespeare's most difficult play."

The report also noted that, "Every actor worthy of his salt wishes to play Hamlet, and presumably Mr. Grant will take the title role, although his talents have, up to date, appeared to best advantage in light comedy."

The idea, however, came to an abrupt end after a professor who had written a modernized version of Shakespeare's tale threatened a lawsuit against Hitchcock's new studio if they moved ahead with his idea. While Hitchcock and Bernstein felt the professor's lawsuit wouldn't hold up in court, the press around the legal action, combined with the other projects Hitchcock had on his plate, and Cary Grant's loss of enthusiasm over the project, left Transatlantic Pictures and Alfred Hitchcock to drop the idea of a modern day *Hamlet*.

eight

THE LOST HITCHCOCKS

"I've often wondered whether I could do a suspense story within a looser film, in a form that's not so tight."

- Alfred Hitchcock

The Bramble Bush

Hitchcock was a man of routine. In real life, he hated suspense and while working he'd call "Cut," at five o'clock. He'd routinely be chauffeured home to dinner with his wife, and by 10 p.m, they'd be in bed sleeping. On Thursdays, however, the couple would go to their favorite restaurant, Chasens, where Hitchcock had his own booth named after him. Once comfortably greeted by the host, and seated in their regular spot, they'd order steak for their adored dogs and Hitch would enjoy wine paired with a rich dinner. It was often during dinner, at home and at Chasens, when the Hitchcocks would discuss his film projects in depth. Alfred would look to Alma as a guide for many of his most important filmmaking decisions.

'The Bramble Bush' was also published under the name 'Worse than Murder' in paperback some markets to promote the suspense.

Alma Reville Hitchcock was clearly more than the wife to Alfred Hitchcock. Although she avoided the spotlight, her ear for witty dialogue and a strong eye for editing and detail made her as much an equal partner in his films than he would ever admit to. She once said, "I was never terribly ambitious," but through her husband she left an indelible mark on film, and was quite possibly the most important figure in helping shape the legacy of Alfred Hitchcock. Alma had a hand in the majority of her husband's films, helping craft the suspense and draw the line that Hitchcock himself often times couldn't draw on his own.

They met while were working together at Paramount's Famous Players-Lasky studio in London, during the early 1920s. She was an up and coming film editor and cinema became their passion. Just a day younger than Alfred, they married on Thursday, December 2, 1926 at a small ceremony in London. It's notable that while Alfred's career on the wedding certificate identifies him as a film director, Alma is identified without an occupation. She would perform the role of wife, as well as sounding board and collaborator. The couple would also have a daughter, Patricia, born on July 7, 1928.

For their honeymoon the couple boarded a train for Paris and headed off to Switzerland and Saint Moritz. A posh vacation spot of ski lodges and resorts catering to millionaires from around the world, the Hitchcocks fell in love with the getaway spot. Arriving via train from Zurich, the locale features expansive skyline views from 6,000 feet above the sea. Their hotel, The Palace Hotel, would be the most luxurious spot they could imagine. Decorated like a French Cathedral, the hotel features 200 miles of ski slopes, bobsled and toboggan runs, ice-skating and sleigh rides.

The Hitchcocks, never known for sport, spent most of their time as tourists and observers with an occasional sleigh ride as the only excursion they would actively participate in. The couple fell so much in love with the spot that they would return to the hotel to celebrate the anniversary of their wedding whenever they could arrange it.

With their 26th wedding anniversary upon them, Alfred and Alma once again returned to Saint Moritz in early December 1952 to celebrate their union. Returning to the Palace Hotel through Christmas, the couple relaxed and regrouped as they prepared for a busy and productive 1953.

While *I Confess* was in post-production and set for release in the early months of 1953, Hitchcock was busy thinking about his next project. It was to be his final film in a four-picture deal with Warner Bros. and was intended to be *The Bramble Bush*, a feature film adaptation of a novel of the same name by David Duncan. Duncan began writing professionally around the age of 33, after working for ten years in government.

Hitchcock's first film for Warner Bros. was actually *Rope* in 1948, but the film was technically a feature for his own production house, Transatlantic Pictures, with Warner Bros. only acting as a distributor for the film. In 1949 he set forth on making *Stage Fright* starring Jane Wyman. It was the first of a four-picture deal with Warner Bros., followed by *Strangers on a Train* in 1951 and *I Confess* in 1953. *The Bramble Bush* would complete the deal.

The Bramble Bush actually started as a concept for Transatlantic Pictures in 1951, with Warner Bros. acting as distributor. In fact, both *I Confess* and *The Bramble Bush* were works in progress during the last half of 1951. Hitchcock was part owner of Transatlantic, giving him added control over his projects, but the company was faltering. Hitchcock kept both films in development and felt that whatever picture reached the point of being most ready for production next would head to the soundstages. Both stories were being crafted simultaneously, but Hitchcock quickly found momentum with *I Confess,* as the idea of a wronged priest implicated in a murder fascinated him.

By the time *I Confess* went into production, Hitchcock had pinned his hopes on *The Bramble Bush* as his next production. While he had numerous other projects in development, the Duncan novel seemed the most promising to be ready in time to begin filming. However, it was dependent on the screenplay. Transatlantic was becoming less and less a player in Hitchcock's production processes and he knew both *I Confess* and *The Bramble Bush* would be better funded as Warner Bros. productions. His ability to afford first-rate stars, excellent locations and the best crews were stronger with a major studio than on his own.

The Bramble Bush is a novel about a soldier of fortune trying to get home from Mexico to San Francisco. He steals another man's passport and changes his identity without realizing that the man is wanted for murder. Originally titled *The Bramble Bush*, the book would be later released under the title *Worse Than Murder* when it was published in mass-market paperback.

For *The Bramble Bush* Hitchcock placed faith in George Tabori, a London journalist who served in the British Army during World War II. Hitchcock first noticed him after his first novel *Original Sin* was produced in 1947 and after his first play *Flight to Egypt* opened on Broadway. In March 1952, he approached him to develop *The Bramble Bush* into a screenplay. Hitchcock had a list of necessary changes to the story including elimination of any "controversial political or economic aspects of the story."

The two men met in Hollywood earlier in the in 1952, with Hitchcock explaining his requirements for the screenplay. Hitchcock wanted the hero's escape from Mexico back to San Francisco to be "clearly motivated." He wanted the end of the film to clearly show the hero innocent and that his return to the key scene of trouble be clearly explained and necessary.

Tabori left the meeting and set forth on writing a suitable screenplay. He had ideas of his own like the hero meeting the villain only to discover he resembled him and decides to steal his passport. He also had the idea that the hero meets the villain's sister, only to have both an attraction and distrust of her. Later, the main character finds he has been set up and framed for murder. He is arrested, escapes, and is hunted by both the police and the villain.

However, when Hitchcock received the completed script he was disappointed with the result. According to letters Hitchcock wrote during the period, he felt Tabori had gone off in a completely different direction. Calling his version "disgraceful."

THE LOST HITCHCOCKS

Of Tabori's efforts, Hitch said he, "ignores everyone's ideas." After what he considered a failure with Tabori, Hitchcock, with help from Alma, attempted to craft his own screenplay for his film. It would be one of the rare occasions where he would attempt such a feat, but it too would be a failure. After weeks of work he still found the story a challenge.

Aside from Tabori's draft of *The Bramble Bush*, and his own failed attempt, Hitchcock also looked to writer Barbara Keon to re-craft the concept, but was still disappointed with the results. He turned to writer William Archibald to see if he could transform it into something usable. Archibald was a playwright, after careers as both a singer and dancer. His play, *The Turn of the Screw*, was a hit in 1950 and Hitchcock hoped for the best. Both Archibald and Tabori worked on *I Confess* and *The Bramble Bush* simultaneously.

Hitchcock turned the Tabori script over to Archibald hoping he might make something of it, but pressure from Warner Bros. was mounting.

Hitch thought Archibald had "sound views of the characters," but was still not convinced he'd have a workable film out of what had been written. Hitchcock still felt he had little more than, "an ordinary chase story," and feared there was no movie coming from the story.

With Warner Bros. pressing him to have a follow-up film to *I Confess* within a year, Hitchcock had to look at all his options, one of which was to drop *The Bramble Bush* in favor of something else.

In late December, Hitchcock cabled Jack Warner to tell him *The Bramble Bush* was proving more difficult than expected and he had other ideas in mind. By January 1953, the director still felt the script had "many weeks of revising" before he might have a feature, but more likely, he suspected, he had to tell Jack Warner, "I cannot lick it and ask them to accept another project."

While in New York in the fall of 1952, Hitchcock saw a play called *Dial M For Murder*. Originally premiering in London, Hitchcock felt the story had strong potential as a film. He noted the idea down as a possibility for a future film concept.

Warner Bros., at the time, felt that the new concept of 3D was a formula it could not afford to miss. With the industry changing, new film processes and the advent of television were causing studios to look toward new technologies and ways to lure viewers to the theater. The new

'The Bramble Bush' would come to the big screen in 1960 in a film version not directed by Hitchcock.

age of 3D began in late 1952 with the release of the first color feature, *Bwana Devil*, was produced. Shot in "Natural Vision," it was a process that was co-created by M. L. Gunzberg. After Gunzberg was unable to convince the major studios to invest he went off on his own, proving it had merit as a revolutionary concept for theaters. Soon studios were all developing the process with Columbia's *Man in the Dark* and Warner Bros. *House of Wax* making the most waves.

Jack Warner was adamant that 3D was the wave of the future and suggested Hitchcock consider the concept for a film of his own. Hitchcock knew *The Bramble Bush* would not transfer well into a 3D film. With location filming in Mexico and San Francisco key to the story, it would be costly and difficult to fit the process into the story in a plausible way. However, Hitchcock remembered seeing *Dial M For Murder* a year earlier and felt the stage play was largely confined to a single set, making it possible to film the story in a way that 3D could be integrated into the film to complement the story.

Around April 1953, Hitchcock asked Warner Bros. if he could drop *The Bramble Bush* and replace it with *Dial M For Murder*. The studio agreed the idea held promise, once Hitch presented the idea of a 3D Hitchcock picture for Warner Bros. Hitchcock gave up the idea of *The Bramble Bush*.

Dial M For Murder would be produced with the 3D process, however, by the time of its release the 3D fad had faded and the expense of releasing the film with the passé concept seemed unnecessary. The film would be released without it and it would be decades before anyone would ever see the 3D version of the feature. *The Bramble Bush* would eventually be released as a film in 1960. Directed by Daniel Petrie, rather than Hitchcock, the film would star Richard Burton, Barbara Rush, Angie Dickinson, and Jack Carson. While *The Bramble Bush* would earn only about $3 million at the box office, Hitchcock's *Dial M For Murder* would pull in more than $6 million, proving the master was right in changing projects.

nine

THE LOST HITCHCOCKS

"I am out to get the best stories I can which will suit the film medium, and I have usually found it necessary to take a hand in writing them myself. I choose crime stories because that is the kind of story I can turn most easily into a successful film. I am ready to use other stories, but I can't find writers who will give them to me in a suitable form."

- Alfred Hitchcock

Wreck of the Mary Deare

In early 1957, at the age of 57, Alfred Hitchcock became ill. On January 17, after a week in bed from weakness, abdominal pains and overall discomfort, the famous director was admitted to Cedars of Lebanon Hospital in Los Angeles to be treated for a hernia. It was a long time

THE LOST HITCHCOCKS

coming. Hitch had suffered with the hernia for years, but ignored it, until the injury finally began causing him severe pains. Surgery was scheduled, and after about 10 days he was resting comfortably at home. During his recovery, Hitchcock read the novel *The Wreck of the Mary Deare* by Hammond Innes and decided it would be his next film.

However, a film was the least of his concerns, when on March 9, at 4 a.m., he was awakened again with severe pains. His wife woke to find him moaning and clutching his chest. After arriving at the hospital, doctors diagnosed a diseased gallbladder, possibly from the large amounts of rich food and fine wine that caused his weight to balloon over the years. More surgery was required, and the director spent another month recuperating at home.

After the success of *To Catch a Thief* in 1955 and *The Man Who*

Hitchcock struggled to find the right story for a film version of 'The Wreck of the Mary Deare.' It would later be filmed without his direction.

Knew Too Much in 1956, Hitchcock was searching for suitable options for his next film. While *The Wrong Man* with Henry Fonda was nearly complete, it was a smaller film, adapted for the screen much like an extended episode of his 1950s television series *Alfred Hitchcock Presents*. It was also a project that completed the terms of a contract with Warner Bros. and Hitchcock had the opportunity to negotiate with various studios for film projects that interested him.

MGM was in need of a hit. That summer the studio's board of directors dropped studio head Dore Schary after roughly eight years in charge, replacing him with producer Sol Siegel. The studio had been losing money for the most of the decade with few hits to write home about, except for a few notable musicals like *Singin' in the Rain, Seven Brides for Seven Brothers* and *Annie Get Your Gun.*

Siegel felt that MGM's shareholders would respond favorably to news that Hitchcock would be on its roster of directors. So much so that Siegel told Lew Wasserman, Hitchcock's agent, that he was willing to offer him his top salary, a huge budget, and a cut of the proceeds if the MGM film was a hit. To sweeten the deal, he even offered to give Hitchcock a clause in his contract providing him rare final cut approval over the finished product.

The Wreck of the Mary Deare was based on the 1956 novel by Hammond Innes and tells the story of the captain of a small rescue ship in the English Channel, who finds a freighter called *The Mary Deare* adrift at sea. The crew seems to have vanished, so as the finder, the captain, thinks he is in line for a large salvage fee. However, before he can take his salvage rights, he discovers the first officer still on board and the officer sends him away. Thus begins a mystery about what happened aboard the Mary Deare and the investigation into the incident that follows.

The novel was optioned by MGM and the plan was to have Alfred Hitchcock direct the film with Gary Cooper as its star. Hitchcock reportedly wanted to work with Cooper, and Hitch was initially interested in the idea. Hitchcock had planned to work with Cooper back in 1940 when he approached him to star in his suspense film *Foreign Correspondent,* but Cooper turned him down, not interested in doing an espionage thriller. When the film became a hit and earned six Academy Award nominations, Cooper later told Hitchcock he regretted not taking him up on his offer.

This time, with Cooper on board, Hitchcock needed help crafting the screenplay. Bernard Herrmann, Hitchcock composer and friend, suggested a friend of his. Ernest Lehman was an up-and-coming contract writer at MGM, and Herrmann thought he might be well suited to help Hitchcock bring the *Mary Deare* project to life. Hitchcock met Lehman at the end of August and the two instantly hit it off over lunch.

While Lehman was busy with several other projects, Hitchcock asked him to read the book and give the idea of a film some thought. Hitchcock too was tied up with his TV series, *Alfred Hitchcock Presents,* and pre-production work on *Vertigo,* to spend any time on the project, but the two agreed to get back together and revisit the concept in the fall.

Hitchcock traditionally directed the opening episode of his TV series and filmed all his introductory and exit monologues in the summer and fall, leaving his winter months open to a feature film. Hitchcock secured Lehman's time for the film, and free moments and long lunches, left him time to work on the MGM production.

With the help of Lehman, Hitch tried for weeks to craft an interesting story out of the tale. Hitch and Lehman reportedly lunched together frequently during the latter half of 1956 and into 1957 to work on the screenplay, but the writer felt his director was more interested in gossip than film talk. "Every time I brought up *The Wreck of the Mary Deare,*" said Lehman, "I saw looks of anxiety cross his face and he adeptly changed the subject."

While the film had elements of both drama and mystery, Hitchcock's trademark suspense was in short supply. Lehman and Hitchcock crafted an opening of the film, his writer recalled. "... a powerful opening image of a ship drifting, deserted, in the English channel," recalled Lehman.

Lehman managed to conjure up a "tentative conclusion" to the film as well, but felt he could do little except insert a handful of flashbacks into the remainder of the film to add any elements of suspense to the film. He said it was doomed to be a "boring courtroom drama."

"I give up. I just cannot see a way of dramatizing this book properly," Lehman finally told Hitchcock. "Please get yourself another writer.

The director ultimately agreed with Lehman, concluding a movie version of the book would be nothing more than a talky, drawn out courtroom drama, so he abandoned the idea, but kept Lehman around. "We get along so well," said Hitchcock, "Let's forget about this one and think of some other picture to do together."

Hitchcock and Lehman continued their long lunches and afternoon meetings, while MGM assumed they were hard at work on *The Wreck of the Mary Deare*. Hitchcock

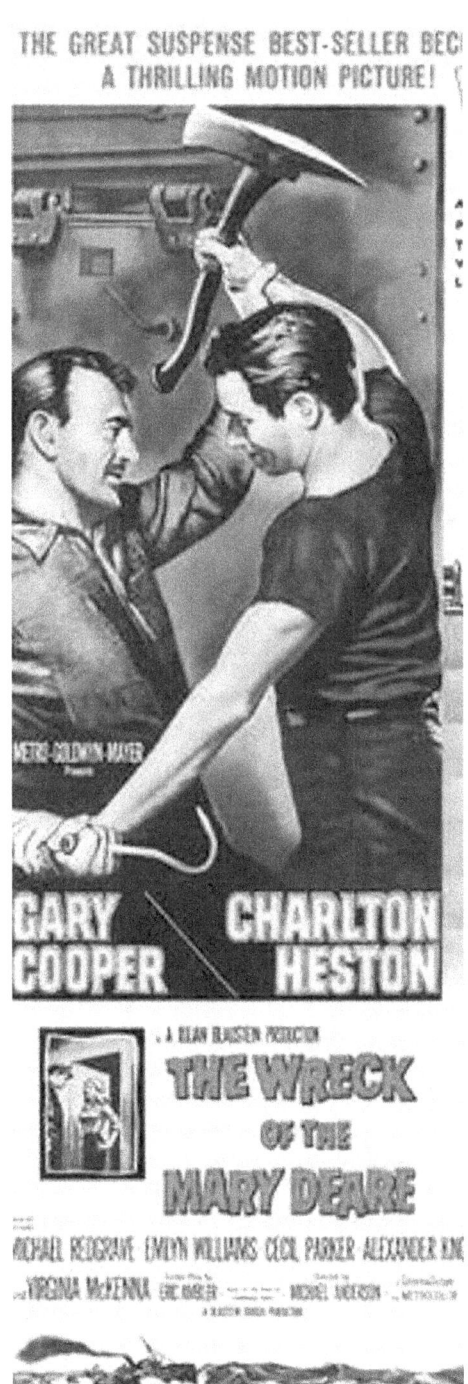

recalled, "... we found it wasn't going to be any good. It belongs to the type of story that's very hard to lick. There's a very famous legend called 'the mystery of the Marie Celeste' ... It's supposed to have happened in the middle of the nineteenth century, when a ship was discovered, in full sail, in the Atlantic. People who boarded the ship found the lifeboats, the galley stove was still hot, and there were remnants of a meal, but no sign of life."

Hitch and Lehman tried for weeks to piece together a picture, but found it lacking. "Why is it that we can't lick this type of story?" asked Hitchcock. "Because it's too strong to begin with. There's so much mystery from the very outset that the attempt to explain it is bound to be terribly laborious. The rest of the story never quite lives up to the beginning."

Hitchcock had hoped that the Innes novel would help him find his way through the mystery, but as a film it simply wouldn't translate for him. "I dropped the idea because it seemed shapeless."

Hitchcock found it difficult to carve out an engaging tale. "Anyway, you have a beautiful set up in that mystery ship with a single man on board. But as soon as you go into explanations, the whole thing becomes very trite, and the public is apt to wonder why you didn't show the events that led up to this point. It's really like picking out a climax and putting it at the beginning."

While Hitch and Lehman kept meeting, in reality the two crafted a synopsis for a new film, tentatively titled "In a Northwesterly Direction."

Hitchcock met with MGM's front office, when asked to report on the progress of his latest film, and he told the studio heads it was going to take him some time to craft a satisfactory film out of the Innes novel. In the meantime, he had another idea in mind, offering his new synopsis to the studio. With the thought that they might get two films from Hitchcock, the studio was thrilled, but Hitch refused to return to *The Wreck of the Mary Dear* and was contractually obligated only to one film, which ultimately became *North by Northwest*. "When you're involved in a project and you see it isn't going to work out, the wisest thing is to simply throw the whole thing away," said Hitchcock.

North by Northwest would be released in July 1959 and would garner both critical and financial success for the director and the studio. *The Wreck of the Mary Deare,* however, would also eventually find its way to the big screen after all when MGM hired writer Eric Ambler to write the screenplay and Michael Anderson to direct Gary Cooper and Charlton Heston in the feature. The film would hit theaters at the very end of 1959, just as Hitchcock was filming *Psycho*. At a cost of roughly $2.5 million the film would take in only about $2.8, barely making a

The film version would be further promoted by a paperback release. Hitchcock dropped the idea when he couldn't find a way to tell the tale with enough suspense.

profit. *North by Northwest*, on the other hand would cost the studio $4.3 and earned a hefty profit, taking in $10 million at the box office and become an instant suspense classic. Hitchcock was right and the film would never achieve the success of *North By Northwest* or *Psycho*.

ten

THE LOST HITCHCOCKS

"As a matter of fact, I don't read about crime in newspapers. The only newspaper I read is the 'London Times,' which is rather dry but has lots of humorous items."

- Alfred Hitchcock

No Bail for the Judge

In April 1959 Alfred Hitchcock boarded a flight for his homeland. Returning to the United Kingdom and familiar London haunts, Hitchcock was in the pre-planning phase of his next film. Like London itself, the film would travel familiar ground for the world famous director, but it would also be a departure of sorts. The film was *No Bail for the Judge*. For starters, it would be a noted departure because its star was not a cool beautiful blonde. Yes, the star could be cool and beautiful, but she was the farthest thing from blonde. She was Audrey Hepburn.

THE LOST HITCHCOCKS

Audrey Hepburn was, in many ways, perfect for a Hitchcock film. While not blonde, her beauty was tempered with an innate comedic ability, as well as an aloofness and coolness that created a charm that made her intensely likeable in even the most awkward of characters. From her early starring roles in *Sabrina* and *Roman Holiday,* she com-

Audrey Hepburn was the intended star of 'No Bail for the Judge.'

manded attention, sometimes at the expense of her leading male counterparts like Humphrey Bogart, William Holden, and Gregory Peck.

In the summer of 1959, just as pre-planning for *No Bail for the Judge* would move into high gear she was at the top of her game again in what some have called one of her finest performance, an Oscar-nominated role as Sister Luke in *A Nun's Story*. She would also win a BAFTA film award as Best British Actress for her performance.

Hepburn was actually filming another movie, *The Unforgiven*, for John Huston and was injured when she was thrown from a horse during a scene in Mexico. She was pregnant at the time and the event caused a scare, as the actress and her husband wanted children very much. Neither she nor her husband, actor Mel Ferrer, wanted her putting herself in any risky situations that might harm their unborn child. After a stay in the hospital, Hepburn was at home recuperating when she received a treatment for Hitchcock's film.

Now, Hepburn initially agreed to star in the Hitchcock film for several obvious reasons. For starters, nearly any actor in Hollywood would agree to star in a Hitchcock film without ever having to look at a script. The famed director was often sought after, and most actors longed for a chance to be directed by the most famous director of the time. Most would sign on, sight-unseen, to anything being planned by him.

In addition, Hitchcock was every bit a women's director and his films offered great challenges for any actress. His female characters often held central roles that were as vital to the story as the male characters in his films. He also lavished great attention on his female leads when it came to costumes, make-up, hair and lighting, and every actress knew she would come off looking her best in front of a Hitchcock camera.

One change the director did want to make was not surprising - he wanted her blonde. Hitchcock hoped to have Audrey dye her hair for the picture so she would continue his theme of golden-haired leading ladies. Hepburn initially told the director she was "looking forward to reading the script," and she would, "do anything he wanted," based on the story he had told her.

THE LOST HITCHCOCKS

By the time Hitch landed in London he was ready for the prep work that was about to begin. He planned to scout the perfect shooting locations for his feature, as well and focus attention on some of the legal aspects of the British court system for some key story elements. To launch his films of the 1960s he need suspense, adventure and romance, but he also needed it to be factual. He certainly wanted to keep in the frame of his most recent work, *North by Northwest*. Even though the film was not yet in theaters, it was turning into something special and many knew it.

Laurence Harvey planned to co-star in 'No Bail for the Judge.'

THE LOST HITCHCOCKS

Herbert Coleman, Henry Bumstead and Samuel Taylor, accompanied Hitchcock on the trip to assist with the research and location scouting. Hitchcock was reportedly agitated at the circus-like atmosphere in Los Angeles International Airport as the wives and children of his traveling companions attended the send-off. However, as the trip commenced he grew excited by the potential the film held. Hitchcock always enjoyed the preparation, scripting nuances, and planning of the shots for his films far more than the actual shooting. He often claimed that by the time the filming was taking place, he had already worked out the entire feature in his head and was no longer interested in the camera work, but only in supervising that the camera capture the scene he had worked out in advance.

One of the many key components of the feature that he had already worked out was the cast of co-stars who would perform alongside Miss Hepburn. John Williams was cast as the central role of the judge while Laurence Harvey would carry the important role of Hepburn's romantic lead as a handsome thief, not unlike Cary Grant's role in *To Catch a Thief.*

John Williams was very much a part of Hitchcock's inner circle of familiar faces, having worked with the director many times. Not only had he starred in 10 episodes of *Alfred Hitchcock Presents*, including *Banco's Chair*, the most recent May 1959 episode directed by Hitchcock himself, but Williams also worked with the director on several of his most notable feature films including *The Paradine Case* in 1947, *Dial M For Murder* in 1954, and *To Catch a Thief* in 1955. He also worked with Audrey Hepburn in *Sabrina* in 1954.

Laurence Harvey, on the other hand was relatively new to working with the likes of Alfred Hitchcock. Harvey had started out in a series of small roles in forgettable films in the late 1940s, but would work steadily through the 50s, never really hitting his stride until *Room at the Top* in 1959 and *Butterfield 8* in 1960. He would also go onto further fame in 1962 opposite Frank Sinatra in the classic *The Manchurian Candidate*. He never worked for Hitchcock before, but after his feature film role fell through he would fulfill his contractual agreement for the director by performing in an episode of *Alfred Hitchcock Presents* in 1959 called *Arthur*. He was a handsome, brooding actor, traits that would suit his character well in *No Bail for the Judge*.

The three lead actors were all initially given a brief treatment of the film with a synopsis of the story and all agreed it sounded like a wonderful feature for Hitchcock and wanted very much to take part in.

Based on a novel of the same name by Henry Cecil, *No Bail for the Judge* centered on a mysterious tale of a capital cases judge in London's Old Bailey Court. The author was actually Henry Cecil Leon, an actual British justice who slightly altered his name for the pen name of the novel. The role of the judge was intended for John Williams.

While walking home one evening the judge falls and hits his head on the pavement after he dodges into the street to save a dog that is nearly run down by a London taxi. He gets up and staggers away from the scene, a bit confused, and is mistaken for drunk by a local prostitute, who takes him home.

The next morning, the judge awakens to discover the prostitute's corpse atop him with a knife protruding from her back. Thinking as a judge, and aiming to do the right thing, he calls the police, but claims he doesn't recall much of the evening. Unsure whether he is guilty of murder, the judge is taken to prison to await trial. His daughter, the role intended for Hepburn, is that of a lawyer who believes her father innocent and sets out to prove it. She heads to her father's home and catches a handsome young thief, Harvey's intended role, but instead of turning him into the police, she agrees to let him go on the grounds that he help her infiltrate London's prostitution underworld, in hopes of solving the crime and finding out who the real murderer is. The couple head off on a dark mission to uncover the truth, and sparks of romance between the two hint at something more.

To be produced by Paramount Pictures, the filming was set to take place in London and be shot in Technicolor and VistaVision. It would herald in the 1960s as Hitchcock's latest masterpiece along the lines of *Vertigo*, a film that offered a lush and colorful, but dark tale set in San Francisco several years earlier. Unlike his black and white films with moody atmosphere, the color film would capture London, as well as Hepburn and Harvey at their best. Contracts were drawn up and casting of Hitchcock's next picture was announced. Before filming could start Audrey Hepburn lost her baby. She headed off to Switzerland to recuperate, still initially intending to film Hitchcock's picture.

One of the challenges Hitchcock faced was in updating the story slightly due to changes in the legal system in Britain in its treatment of prostitution. Ernest Lehman was originally tasked with the job of writing the screenplay for the film but eventually removed himself from the picture because he had misgivings about the story. Samuel Taylor took over the writing responsibilities and focused on making the story more plausible.

The feature also needed enough action and suspense peppered throughout the story to keeping moviegoers focused on the mystery at hand. Hitchcock was not as interested in they mystery, but rather in the suspense, the action and a leading lady in peril.

Hitchcock arranged for Taylor to spend some time getting the realities of the story first hand by talking to a prostitute who had changed careers and was now working as a London secretary. Meeting at the Paramount offices in London, Taylor got an earful about the lively London sex trade. He was then required to recount all the tales verbatim for Hitchcock, who was captivated by the lurid sexuality of it all.

In one of the climactic sequences intended to capture some of the darker underbelly of world of prostitution and the dramatic story behind the film, Taylor added a scene where the leading lady is dragged into London's Hyde Park and nearly raped by her assailant, before being rescued.

By late May, Hitchcock and his traveling companions returned to Los Angeles with the major elements worked out. The entire tale was committed to paper, with nearly every scene and line of dialogue worked out. A final script soon was completed and ready for the actors shortly to begin shooting Hitchcock's picture.

As *A Nun's Story* was doing big box office and acclaim for its star was rolling in, Audrey Hepburn received the script for her next picture and cringed at the idea of being raped on film for theater audiences to see. Even though the scene was to be done discretely and with little emotional anguish to the star, Hepburn was reluctant to expose herself to such a scene. In fact she and her husband had been planning to try again for a child and the actress had no intention of putting herself or a child she expected to be carrying in danger by being dragged around a movie set or in the real Hyde Park. Hepburn would find out she was pregnant in the fall of 1958, and had she agreed to do the film would have had to endure the terrible treatment Hitchcock had planned for her while pregnant.

Audrey Hepburn declined to appear in *No Bail for the Judge* and Hitchcock hit the roof. He was beside himself with anger. He had already spent approximately $200,000 preparing for the film and to lose his star caused him great discomfort. In fact, at this stage he actually lost all interest in the film and told Paramount it would be better for them to cut their losses now rather than invest another $3 million in a film he no longer wanted to make.

To add insult to injury Hitchcock's *North by Northwest* had to delay its release because *A Nun's Story* was being extended at movie houses across the United States. Then to top it off, he lost first prize award at both The San Sebastian International Film Festival and The Venice Film Festival to *A Nun's Story*.

He would never forgive Audrey Hepburn for walking away from him. Some suggest he as much as "hated her" after dropping the film. He had grown very frustrated with female stars that abandon him for husbands and children. Grace Kelly and Vera Miles had both caused him great anguish by allowing marriage or pregnancy to get in the way of his work and Audrey Hepburn didn't help matters. However, Hitchcock gave interviews in the 1961 timeframe that suggested he still hoped he might get *No Bail for the Judge* back off the ground with Hepburn and Harvey as its stars, but nothing serious ever came from it.

Hepburn would go on to film a very successful "Hitchcockian" feature several years later, with Cary Grant no less. The film was *Charade*. Audrey Hepburn would work with Hitch, sort of in 1966, when she filmed a scene in *How to Steal a Million* reading an Alfred Hitchcock paperback.

Hitchcock still had a film to deliver to Paramount for 1960. The problem was solved when he picked up a copy of a little novel by Robert Bloch's called *Psycho*.

THE LOST HITCHCOCKS

eleven

THE LOST HITCHCOCKS

"Technique should enrich the action. One doesn't set the camera at a certain angle just because the cameraman happens to be enthusiastic about that spot. The only thing that matters is whether the installation of the camera at a given angle is going to give the scene its maximum impact."

- Alfred Hitchcock

Thunderball

After the release of Ian Fleming's eighth James Bond novel in 1961, producers Harry Saltzman and Albert R. "Cubby" Broccoli set their sights on turning its story into a film. They created a studio called Eon Productions with the hope of bringing the new novel, *Thunderball*, to the big screen. However, in looking into acquiring the rights to the Fleming story, they found a complex legal case that needed untangling before the film could be made.

Originally intended as the first film in the James Bond franchise, *Thunderball* wouldn't hit movie screens until 1965, with Saltzman and Broccoli opting to take *Dr. No* to the big screen as the first Bond movie in the long-running film series. What many were unaware of was that Alfred Hitchcock was the desired director for the first installment of Bond, as director of *Thunderball*.

Writer of the James Bond novels, Ian Fleming.

THE LOST HITCHCOCKS

It was back in the fall of 1958 when Ivar Bryce introduced a young Irish writer and director named Kevin McClory, to his friend, Ian Fleming. Fleming had been thinking about his Bond novels as films and McClory's skills could prove useful. The three men, along with Bryce's friend Ernest Cuneo, created a partnership called Xanadu Productions, and over a series of months, they crafted the concept for a film initially entitled *Longitude 78 West*. A host of outlines and scripts followed, along with a number of possible film titles. "SPECTRE," "James Bond of the Secret Service," "James Bond, Secret Agent," and "Thunderball" were suggested.

Xanadu was never legally formed into a company and after McClory's film, *The Boy and the Bridge*, was released in July 1959, and was badly received by critics and moviegoers, Fleming lost interest in McClory as a potential Bond film director. In fact, Fleming thought it would be much more interesting if he could get Alfred Hitchcock to make the first film version of a Bond novel.

In September 1959 Fleming sent a telegram to novelist Eric Ambler, a mutual friend of both Fleming and Hitch, suggesting Hitchcock as the director of *Thunderball*. Ambler was the husband of Joan Harrison, a key member of Hitchcock's inner creative team. Harrison was a screenwriter and producer who started as Hitchcock's secretary in 1933 and over the years became an important sounding board in the development and production of his films and TV series. Hitchcock struck up a friendship with Ambler after his wedding to Harrison in 1958.

Outlining the plot for Ambler, Fleming's telegram inquired, "Would Hitchcock be interested?"

The telegram explained the concept to Ambler, writing, "Have written Bond movie treatment featuring Mafia stolen atomic bomber blackmail of England culminating Nassau with extensive underwater dramatics."

The telegram followed up by elaborating on the project, "This is for my friend Ivar Bryce's Xanadu Films Ltd., which recently completed *Boy and Bridge*, England's choice for Venice festival, but blasted by critics and flop at Curzon though now doing excellently on pre-release Rank circuit."

Fleming then inquired specifically, "Would Hitchcock be interested in directing this first Bond film in association with Xanadu?"

The telegram ended by adding, "Plentiful finance available. This purely old boy enquiry without involvement but think we might all have a winner particularly if you were conceivably interested in scripting."

Sent in September 1959, Fleming never disclosed the actual name of the film, and he would actually settle on the name *Thunderball* most likely after the telegram was sent. Some suggest that Fleming had Hitchcock so much in mind as director, that his screenplay concept was adjusted so James Bond came off as more, "Hitchcock-friendly." Fleming's film secret agent was adjusted from the "ruthless, sadistic and misogynistic" man in the novels to a, "suave character who was keen on women and affairs." It was suspected that the screenwriters were influenced Hitchcock's lead character *North by Northwest* - Roger Thornhill - played by Cary Grant.

By January 1960, during a visit from McClory at Fleming's Jamaican home Goldeneye, Fleming told the director he planned to send the screenplay to MCA. Hitchcock had been under representation from MCA since 1945, with Lew Wasserman acting as his agent. Making a deal with MCA would have further helped align the Bond film with Hitchcock's directing skills. Fleming assured McClory that he'd suggest MCA provide both Bryce and McClory producer credit, but if MCA "was unwilling," McClory would be encouraged to either sell his portion of the film to MCA, or take them to court.

No records indicate MCA ever considered financing the Bond picture, but Fleming reportedly hoped to get *Thunderball* into production in 1960 with Richard Burton as James Bond and Alfred Hitchcock directing. The screenplay, though, went nowhere that year. With McClory unable to raise finances to get his version into production, Fleming decided to return to what he knew best. Back at his Goldeneye estate in Jamaica, Fleming repurposed much of the screenplay into the novel he titled *Thunderball*. This led to Kevin McClory and Jack Whittingham to sue the author for breach of copyright.

The novel *Thunderball* was completed between January and March of 1960 and released to the public on March 27, 1961. After the book's release, Saltzman and Broccoli acquired the screen rights for the film. Saltzman and Broccoli didn't have any strong contacts at MCA, but Broccoli had been part owner of a small British studio called Warwick Films, back in the 1950s. Through his work at Warwick, Broccoli had a connection with Arthur Krim, head of United Artists. This helped open

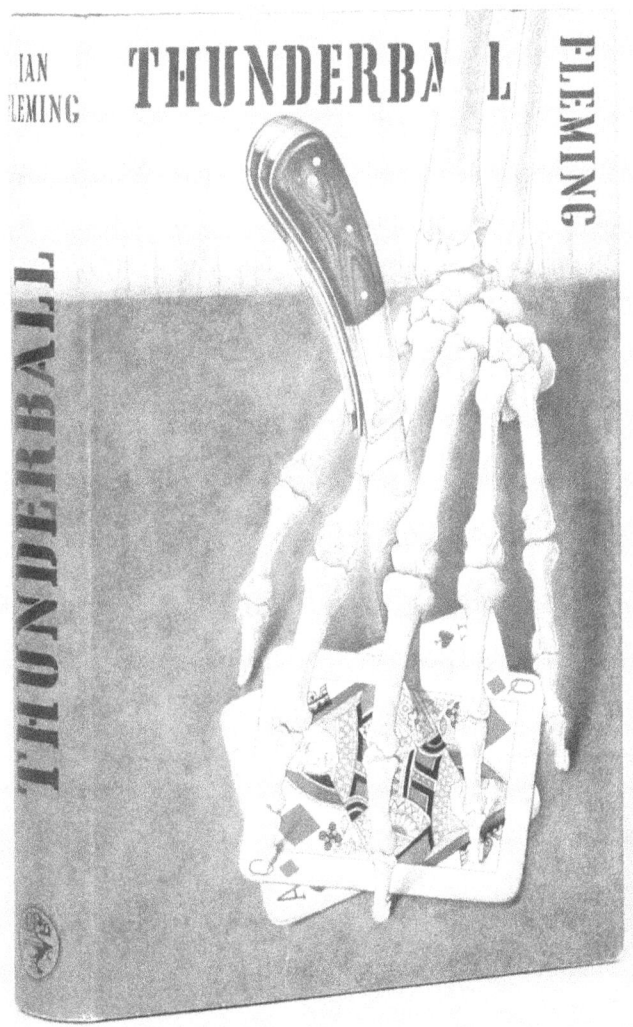

the door for Eon to secure financing of $1 million to make the first Bond feature film, *Thunderball*.

However, after McClory read an advance copy of the book, he and Whittingham, a writer who worked on the screenplay, turned to the London Court's for an injunction to stop the publication of *Thunderball*. A case of plagiarism was heard in March 1961 and found the book could be published.

Fearing legal actions against the story of *Thunderball*, Eon did a quick reassessment of the situation, with Saltzman and Broccoli selecting *Dr. No*, Fleming's sixth novel, as the best option for the first Bond picture.

McClory continued to pursue Fleming in court and again sued him in November 1963. The case of *McClory v. Fleming* was heard over three weeks, during which time Fleming suffered a heart attack.

In failing health Fleming offered a deal to McClory. Settling out of court, Fleming gave McClory literary and film rights for the screenplay version of *Thunderball*, with Fleming retaining the rights to the novel. Nine months after the settlement on August 12, 1964, Ian Fleming died following another heart attack. He was 56 and left behind a legacy of James Bond stories.

Dr. No was released in October 1962. Directed by Terence Young, the film pulled in more than $6 million worldwide, making it a bonafide hit, off the $1 million budget. *Thunderball* was eventually completed and released in 1965, after Fleming's death and with McClory listed in a producer role. It would be a surefire box office smash, helping launch the Bond phenomenon and secure the franchise at the box-office. So much so, that it remains the most successful Bond film when taking inflation into account. Its leading man, Sean Connery, would become a superstar as the debonair secret agent.

Had he been offered the opportunity through MCA, Hitchcock may have considered the project. However, no response from Hitchcock has been noted, but reports suggest that Hitchcock was an avid reader of Fleming's work and back in the early 1950s talked about the idea of

THE LOST HITCHCOCKS

bringing Bond to the big screen. Some reports suggest that Hitch toyed with the idea of making a film version of Fleming's 1953 novel, *Casino Royale*, but after the story ended up as a teleplay on CBS in 1954, the director dropped the idea.

Interestingly enough, a few years after the *Casino Royale* TV debut, CBS proposed a James Bond television series based on Fleming's stories. Fleming even reportedly drafted as many as seven outlines before CBS dropped the project. Hitchcock, in the meantime, would succeed with his own CBS series, *Alfred Hitchcock Presents*, debuting on the network in the fall of 1955.

As for films, after *Dr. No*, Bond would become one of the most financially successful and longest running franchises in movie history. Hitchcock had his own plethora of movie ideas landing on his desk. In fact, he'd reportedly spread them out across the top of his desk in his production office as he reviewed them all, discussing them and trying to

Writer Ian Fleming hoped to entice Alfred Hitchcock to turn 'Thunderball' into the first James Bond feature film,

determine which one had the most potential.

Sean Connery quickly became concerned about being typecast as James Bond and was eager for other opportunities to stretch as an actor. Hitchcock considered him for the role of Mitch Brenner in *The Birds*, but eventually selected Rod Taylor for the role instead, because Connery was tied up with his latest Bond effort. After the release of *The Birds* in 1963, Hitchcock would turn his attentions to a dramatic mystery called *Marnie*. When it came time to cast his leading man, who better than James Bond himself. Sean Connery would ultimately be directed by Hitchcock, after all, in 1964's *Marnie*.

THE LOST HITCHCOCKS

twelve

THE LOST HITCHCOCKS

"I could do a whole script myself, but I'm too lazy to do that, or too preoccupied in other directions. That's why I bring in other writers. But I suppose that the films with suspense and atmosphere are, to some degree, my creations as a writer."

- Alfred Hitchcock

The Blind Man

In many ways James Stewart was the quintessential Hitchcock leading man. Having starred in four of the director's best-known films, he brought life to Hitchcock's common man catapulted into the most uncommon of situations. It was what Hitchcock strived to achieve with nearly all his films, and working with Stewart made it all the easier. Even his name, commonly referred to as simply "Jimmy," made moviegoers like and identify with him. Hitchcock saw this and exploited it for what it allowed him to achieve on the big screen. Hitchcock knew familar names and faces helped moviegoers to become attached to his characters without him having to write it into the script.

Jimmy Stewart was the intended star of Hitchcock's 'The Blind Man, but the film would never be completed.

For *Rope,* in 1948, Stewart's character becomes engaged in a battle of wits, as a pair of killers attempt to get away with the perfect murder. It's up to Stewart, their former schoolteacher, to prove there is no such thing.

Rear Window, in 1954, put Stewart in a wheelchair, immobilizing him in his apartment. Out of boredom he finds himself watching his neighbors to pass the time. When he thinks one of them has killed his wife, a cat and mouse thriller begins with Stewart trying to prove he's right and not become the killer's next victim. The film earned Hitchcock a nomination for Best Director.

Stewart returned in 1956 in *The Man Who Knew Too Much.* This time as a family doctor traveling with his family through Morocco when he stumbles upon an international assassination plot, putting his family in jeopardy as he struggles to save his son and stop the villains from realizing their evil plot.

Lastly, *Vertigo,* in 1958, would arguably be Hitchcock's crowning cinematic achievement as Stewart is set up to be the witness to a suicide that's actually a murder. As a retired San Francisco detective, suffering from acrophobia, he becomes obsessed with the dead wife of an old friend and discovers that things are not always what they seem.

Hitchcock and Stewart remained friends after the completion of *Vertigo,* but both men moved on to other projects. Hitchcock was off to *North By Northwest* with Cary Grant, while Stewart reteamed with *Vertigo* co-star Kim Novak for *Bell, Book and Candle.*

However, after the success of *Psycho*, Hitchcock began looking for his next project and he knew it had to be a good one. *Psycho* had earned the director another nomination for the Academy Award for Best Director, and although he would lose the coveted statuette, *Psycho* would be his biggest financial success. Filmed on a low budget of little more than $800,000 the film earned more than $6 million during the summer it premiered and an estimated $11 million over the course of its initial run. The shocking twists and turns had everyone talking and Hitchcock knew he had his work cut out for him in coming up with a follow-up.

THE LOST HITCHCOCKS

Hitchcock spent a large part of 1961 on the release of *Psycho* in the international markets. He oversaw advertising campaigns, premiere dates, and even the dubbing of dialogue into other languages. His tour took him to Hong Kong in January 1961; followed by Argentina in March; Spain in April; Denmark, Uruguay and Greece in May; Ireland in in July; and Brazil in November, and would be followed by more releases in 1962. While the film's popularity ensured success at the box office and kept the director busy, he knew he'd need to look ahead to the next film to stay in the game. Universal was eager to get him back behind the camera.

Reports suggest that for nearly a year after *Psycho*'s release Hitchcock still had not come up with a concept to follow up his most successful film. In the fall, he focused on the 1961-62 season of *Alfred Hitchcock Presents*, for which he would direct two episodes. He also was involved in a host of meetings with Paramount over his impending move to Universal. While the move would officially take place in 1962 the relocation to the largest bungalow on Universal's lot would also include relocation of offices for his design staff, writer and his assistant. The move would involve writing equipment, a production room, private meeting spaces and everything that might go along with the director's vast enterprise of film, television, records, books, magazines and other efforts that carried the Hitchcock name.

Several film projects were garnering the director's attention that year. He would spread out the outlines of the stories across his desk and consider each, as he tried to hone in on the one with the most promise and kept others moving along in the background. One film that held promise was an original story called "The Blind Man."

For Hitchcock, the casting process often began immediately. If it wasn't done before the film's conception it was almost always complete before production began. Casting was an important task for the director and was done well in advance of pre-production whenever possible. For both Cary Grant and Jimmy Stewart, Hitch knew who his stars were before any work on the film actually started. This often helped him tailor dialogue, scenes and storyboards with his star in mind.

While a star like Jimmy Stewart knew who he was working for, when casting began for other actors, there was more ambiguity, certainly as the director's name became more an more well known. "Hitchcock was very organized and very particular," recalled script supervisor and special assistant Peggy Robertson. "We often would try to keep his name out of the preliminary casting, because once an agent learned he was dealing with Hitchcock, the actor's price would begin to climb."

Once casting was set and production began Hitchcock's name could open doors for location shooting and key production crew who enjoyed the nobility of being a part of a Hitchcock picture. But that was not always the case. Often financial details and key production requirements could cause a film concept to derail. Such is the case with Hitchcock's *The Blind Man*.

In mid-summer 1960 Hitchcock met with Ernest Lehman about an original story for a film called *The Blind Man*. It would star Jimmy Stewart, who would be paid a percentage of the film's profits, and was interested in the idea of working with Hitchcock again. Stewart was working on two films for director John Ford, *Two Rode Together* and *The Man Who Shot Liberty Valance*, at the time and the experience was anything but delightful. Ford was a difficult director, and Stewart was warned about Ford's aggressive behavior by both John Wayne and Henry Fonda, but ignored the warnings. Stewart found working with Ford difficult because he wasn't very forthcoming on his direction and Stewart felt he was often "left in the dark."

After *Two Rode Together* was released in July 1961, Stewart was back in the saddle for the follow up film, but considered a return to the more comfortable surroundings of a Hitchcock film, a welcoming thought. However, first the story would have to be worked out. Stewart was making roughly $200,000 per picture around this time, but like many other name stars, he also earned a cut of the proceeds, encouraging him to select projects that would do well at the box office, and those he would promote to help them succeed.

THE LOST HITCHCOCKS

Ernest Lehman's original screenplay concept was a simple one. A blind man, played by Stewart, regains his eyesight after receiving the eyes of a dead man. However, all is not what it seems when the man begins to have "strange memories and disturbing feelings toward a man he meets who proves to be the murderer of his doctor."

As the story developed, Lehman fleshed out Stewart's character as a famous blind jazz pianist named Jimmy Shearing, who undergoes a radical medical procedure to obtain an eye transplant. The operation turns out to be a success, however, it comes with some strange side effects. His new eyes happen to be those of a murdered man, and captured on the retina of his new eyes are images of the murderer. The jazz man, along with help from his nurse and love interest, Jenny, begin a cat and mouse chase to track down the killer – hopefully, before someone else becomes his next victim.

Lehman signed a contract in December 1960 to craft the story for a Hitchcock film. The main character was to be based on the life of musician George Shearing. Born in London in 1919, Shearing was congenitally blind and had little formal musical education, but developed his skills by playing piano in a neighborhood pub. After joining an all-blind band in the 1930's he found success and arrived in America in 1947 where he established himself as a preeminent jazz musician. His U.S. reputation grew after he was booked into Birdland, the legendary jazz spot in New York. Lehman and Hitchcock used his, "up-from-the-bootstraps" story as the basis for the character and combined his last name with Stewart's first name for the suggested character's possible name – Jimmy Shearing.

Hitchcock envisioned several key scenes he planned to storyboard out. One scene was a cat and mouse chase aboard the ocean liner, RMS Queen Mary, and another takes place in Covent Garden where Hitchcock wanted opera singer Maria Callas to, "witness a murder while onstage singing." Callas' high note in the song would become, "a scream which the audience applauds," according to Lehman.

The story would end "with the heavy tossing acid in Jimmy's face and dies, blinding him for life, and he winds up just where he started," said Lehman.

The concept progressed when Hitchcock and Lehman had time, but began to unravel as the year progressed. One key scene was to have taken place at Disneyland and it became one of the big moments in

Walt Disney objected to 'Psycho' and refused to allow Hitchcock the use of Disneyland to film 'The Blind Man.'

Hitchcock's vision for the film. While watching a Wild West show at Disneyland with his family, Shearing was to begin having visions of being shot. The emotional scene would cause him to discover that through dead man's eyes he was witnessing his murder. The image of dead man's killer was still imprinted on the retina of his new eyes. The killer would then have to kill Shearing to avoid being caught.

The climactic scene became impossible when Walt Disney refused to allow Hitchcock to shoot location footage from inside the gates of Disneyland. After the release of *Psycho,* Walt Disney reportedly called the film "disgusting" and wouldn't permit his children to watch *Psycho.* He also didn't feel his family theme park would be an appropriate backdrop for the likes of and Alfred Hitchcock film.

Then, when Stewart backed out of the project because of other commitments, the lead character simply was referred to as "a David Niven type" and Hitchcock began to lose interest in the concept. Lehman struggled with the script, reportedly unable to solve some of the key plot angles, and eventually arrived at Hitchcock's office one afternoon, announcing he was quitting the project. Hitchcock was furious and reportedly vowed never to work with Lehman again.

"One of my problems with writers," Hitchcock said, "is that when you tell them it is going to be a murder story, they start thinking in low-key terms. That is not my method. I think murder should be done on a lovely summer's day by a babbling brook. The liveliest fellow at a party might well be a psychopathic killer."

Without a capable writer, and the unwillingness of Walt Disney to give Hitchcock the perfect location for his story, the director cancelled his plans for the film, and *The Blind Man* was never completed.

Hitchcock considered two other projects to replace *The Blind Man* in 1962 when he told reporters he was considering a film version of the French play, *Trap for a Solitary Man.* It's about a wife who disappears while on holiday in the French Alps. When she returns she finds that her husband does not recognize her. He also considered making *Village of Stars*, a film version of a novel about a pilot who is stuck in the air with an atomic bomb that is rigged to go off when he reaches a low altitude. Neither idea went very far.

Hitchcock did, however, call on Walt Disney for magic in his next film. The director used a special Disney camera and hired Disney animation and special effects artist, Ub Iwerks, co-creator of Mickey Mouse, to help design bird attacks used in his 1963 film *The Birds*.

THE LOST HITCHCOCKS

thirteen

THE LOST HITCHCOCKS

"It's not really Hitchcock material. What bothers me is the ghost,"
— **Alfred Hitchcock**

A Ghost Story by Alfred Hitchcock: Mary Rose

Back in 1920, while living in London and still very early in his career, Alfred Hitchcock spent a great deal of time at the theater. In fact, during these years, he saw nearly every major stage play to hit London. It would be several years before he would begin directing his collection of legendary films, but as a member of the crew on a handful of silent films, and as a would-be storyteller, Hitchcock was immersed in the British entertainment industry, learning all he could.

That year he saw a play called *Mary Rose* at London's Haymarket Theatre. It starred a young woman named Fay Compton who Hitch would later work with on his first and only attempt at a musical, *Waltzes of Vienna,* when he cast her as a countess. *Mary Rose* was written by James M. Barrie and would be revived several more times, in 1926, 1929, again in 1951, and even more recently in 2007. Hitchcock found himself taken with the story.

The lead character, Mary Rose, is a teenager when the play opens. She lives at home with her parents, but shortly after the story begins, a man named Simon comes to her home to ask her parents for

Hitchcock intended for Tippi Hedren to star as 'Mary Rose.'

their daughter's hand in marriage. Her parents, Mr. and Mrs. Morley, approve the union but only after explaining to Simon that Mary is "a little different." They tell him that some years earlier, while on vacation in Scotland's Outer Herbides, Mary disappeared. Her father was fishing while Mary was quietly sketching not far away. When he looked back for her after a few moments she was suddenly gone. They looked everywhere for her, but she was nowhere to be found. Thirty days later she reappeared. She had no recollection of having been gone for 30 days and believed that no more than a few hours had passed for her.

    The family returned home, but Mary seemed slightly different to them. They could not quite put their finger on it, but her mother explains it to Simon by saying, "I have sometimes thought that our girl is curiously young for her age – as if – you know, how just a touch of frost may stop the growth of a plant and yet leave it blooming – it has sometimes seemed to me that a cold finger had once touched my Mary Rose."

    Unconcerned about the story, Simon responds by saying, "What you are worrying about is just her innocence - which seems a holy thing to me." He still very much wishes to marry the young girl and the wedding goes forward. About five years later, a married Mary and Simon return to the island with their young son and Mary once again disappears. Mary eventually returns, but this time it's more than 25 years later. Strangely enough, in her return she appears not to have aged more than a day. Her parents and husband, much older now, are confused, as is Mary. Because she believes no time has passed, she expects her three-year-old son to still be a small child, but he, in fact, is a grown man. The son, named Harry, is apparently also now missing. In the original version of the story it is suggested that he is a prisoner of war during World War I.

    Harry eventually resurfaces and returns to his childhood home many years later only to find a ghost inhabits the house. He soon discovers that the ghost is that of his mother, Mary, and the two finally meet again and have a long and touching reunion that sets her free from her ghostly wanderings. She can then return to the island for eternity.

    After seeing the play Hitchcock was captivated by the mysterious nature of the tale and felt the story would make a fine film. He carried the idea with him for many years, eventually buying the screen rights to the play, and in the late 1950s and early 1960s began to work on the idea as a feature film. In fact, it was 1963 that he sought out Fay Compton, star of the original theatrical version he saw in 1920, hoping to possibly cast her in one of the roles in his film, as Mary's aged mother.

He hired Jay Presson Allen, the writer who helped breath life into *Marnie,* to craft the screen version of the play. A first draft offered Hitchcock the bones of the story and he complemented them with his own ideas for Presson Allen to incorporate into a second draft that she delivered to the director by Valentine's Day 1964.

Albert Whitlock, a longtime collaborator of Hitchcock's was contracted for a number of "sketches" of scenes for the would-be film. Hitchcock once told Whitlock his concept behind the film was to center on the ghostly aspects of Barrie's original story. Hitchcock told him that the film would not be promoted as, "Hitchcock's Mary Rose," but as, "A Ghost Story by Alfred Hitchcock: Mary Rose." "That'll get 'em," Hitchcock suggested.

Hitchcock had, at one time, reportedly hoped to have Grace Kelly take on the role of Mary Rose and then later set his hopes on his leading lady of *The Birds* and *Marnie*, Tippi Hedren, as the cool beautiful star of the film. But before *Marnie* could make it to the theaters, Hedren and Hitchcock would have a falling out. Hedren was dropped as the would-be star of his upcoming *Mary Rose.*

However, Hitch didn't entirely abandon *Mary Rose* once Hedren was dropped from the project. Initially, he kept hope alive of doing the film with another actress. Claire Griswold, was reportedly suggested as his other potential star of the film. The bulk of Griswold's body of work was in television. She would have guest roles on many television dramas in the late 50s and early 60s, including *The DuPont Show of the Month, Perry Mason, The Dick Powell Show* and *The Twilight Zone.* In addition, she would come to Hitchcock's attention through two performances in his TV series, one in 1962, and another in 1963. She too, like Tippi

Hedren, would be put through elaborate screen tests, filming scenes from *To Catch a Thief*.

He described his upcoming film to *The Times of London* during a visit to the United Kingdom in 1964 as, "The island that likes to be visited. 'I see it essentially as a horror story.' To hear him describing effects he has in mind for the latter, like having the semi-phantom *Mary Rose* lit from inside, so that she casts a ghostly glow instead of a shadow on the walls, and in a death scene letting her husband feel her brow when

Tippi Hedren would be dropped from 'Mary Rose' after an incident with the director.

she goes into a trance and finds his hand covered in blue powder, 'I don't know exactly what it signifies, but I like the idea,' one is left in no doubt that he starts his films very much from the visual end of things."

However, the film was not to be. Claire Griswold, like Grace Kelly, Audrey Hepburn and Vera Miles, would disappoint the director when she chose husband and family over stardom. She would announce her pregnancy before further details of the film could be finalized. He was not pleased.

In addition, the disappointment of *Marnie* left Universal feeling less than enthusiastic about the screenplay of *Mary Rose*. There were too many similarities in the mood and style of the film. The screenplay, some have said, left out too many ghostly scares that might make for good box office. His horror efforts like *Psycho* and *The Birds* centered on the horrific to sell the pictures and without that his fans were often left disappointed. Lew Wasserman, the key figure at Universal, an ardent supporter of Hitchcock, wasn't convinced the film would make money.

Hitchcock still felt his reputation alone would help him see the film through and his hopes were boosted when The Screen Producers Guild gave him with their Milestone Award in 1965. Even though *Marnie* had suffered in both reviews and at the box office his renowned as a director still earned him a great deal of respect and admiration. But Universal wasn't about to bankroll another failed experiment, no matter how much of an icon Alfred Hitchcock was, and his plans for the film languished.

Hitchcock would later say in interviews that his contract with Universal allowed him to make any film, "so long as it cost under $3 million, and so long as it wasn't *Mary Rose.*" But he never stopped thinking about his film version of the story. Hitchcock would detail his idea of the film to Francois Truffaut during his series of interviews in the mid 1960s, calling it, "a little like a science-fiction story."

"If I were to make the film, I would put the girl in a dark-gray dress and I would put a neon tube of light inside, around the bottom of the dress, so that the light would only hit the heroine. Whenever she moved, there would be no shadow on the wall, only a blue light. You'd have to create the impression of photographing a presence rather than a body. At times she would appear very small in the image, at times very big. She wouldn't be a solid lump, you see, but rather like a sensation. In this way you lose the feeling of real space and time. You should be feeling that you are in the presence of an ephemeral thing, you see."

"It's a lovely subject," commented Truffaut. "Also a sad one."

"Yes, very sad," Hitchcock agreed. "Because the real theme is: If the dead were to come back, what would you do with them?"

Hitchcock continued to believe in the film, telling Truffaut, "I still haven't definitely dropped the idea of making it. A few years back it might have seemed that the story would be too irrational for the public. But since then the public's been exposed to these twilight-zone stories, especially on television …"

In fact, Hitchcock kept the idea of filming *Mary Rose* with him until his death. His estate held the screen rights to the play until 1987, many years after his death.

Hitchcock branded himself in print with a series of successful paperback books from Dell Publishing.

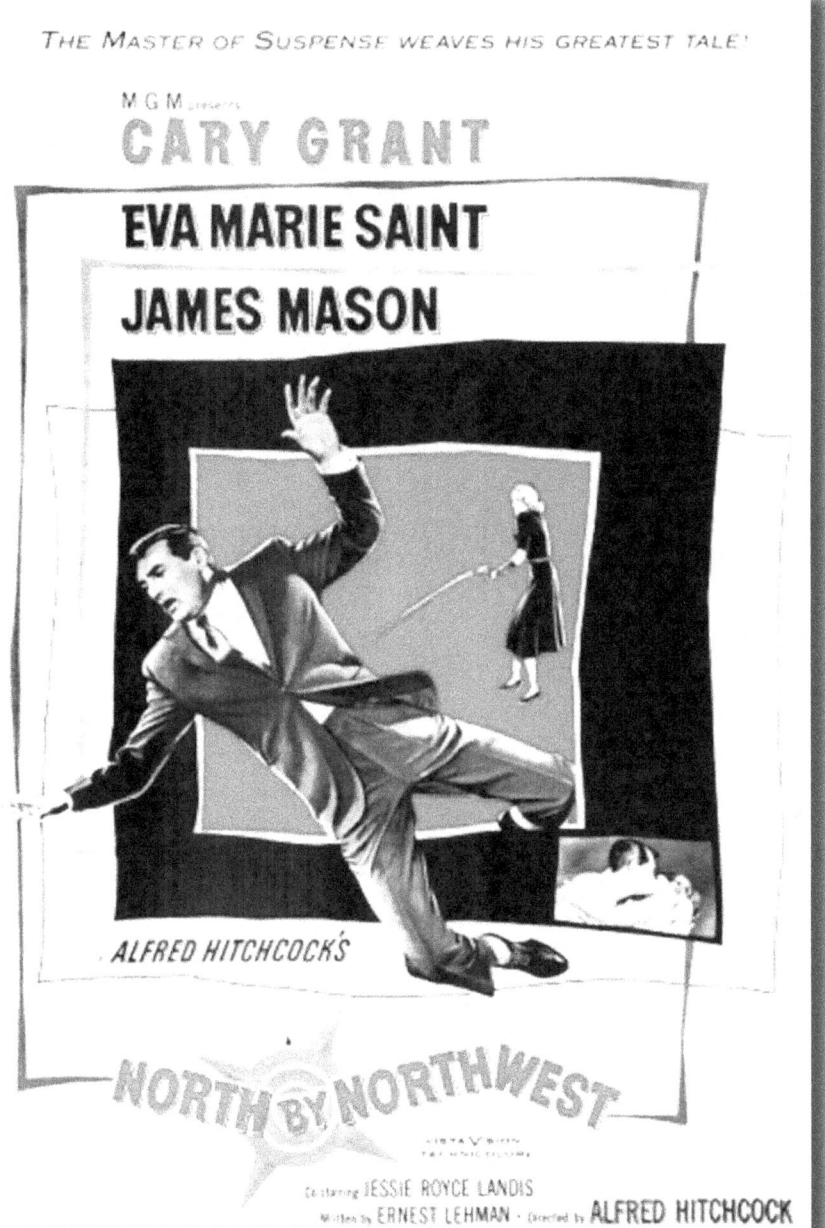

'North by Northwest' in 1959 starring Cary Grant and Eva Marie Saint would become one of the director's most financially successful and critically-acclaimed films and would end the 1950s on a high note, but the director struggled as he looked for a suitable follow-up feature.

THE LOST HITCHCOCKS

By the 60s Hitchcock was so recognizable that he became the focal point of much of the promotion of his film releases.

Janet Leigh served as the star of 'Psycho,' (above) in promotional material to put viewers off upon her death in the film. Leigh, (left), recalled that numerous stuffed "mother" corpses, (right) were considered and used in the film.

Janet Leigh's famous shower scene was filmed over the course of seven days. In later years Leigh would claim she continued to receive odd death threats that stemmed from the scene.

The release of 'Psycho' in June 1960 was a blockbuster. Theaters (above) were sold out and long lines formed as patrons waited for their chance to see what Hitchcock had created. The infamous house (right) was a set Hitchcock created to offer the eerie home for Norman Bates and his mother. The house remained on the Universal backlot for many years.

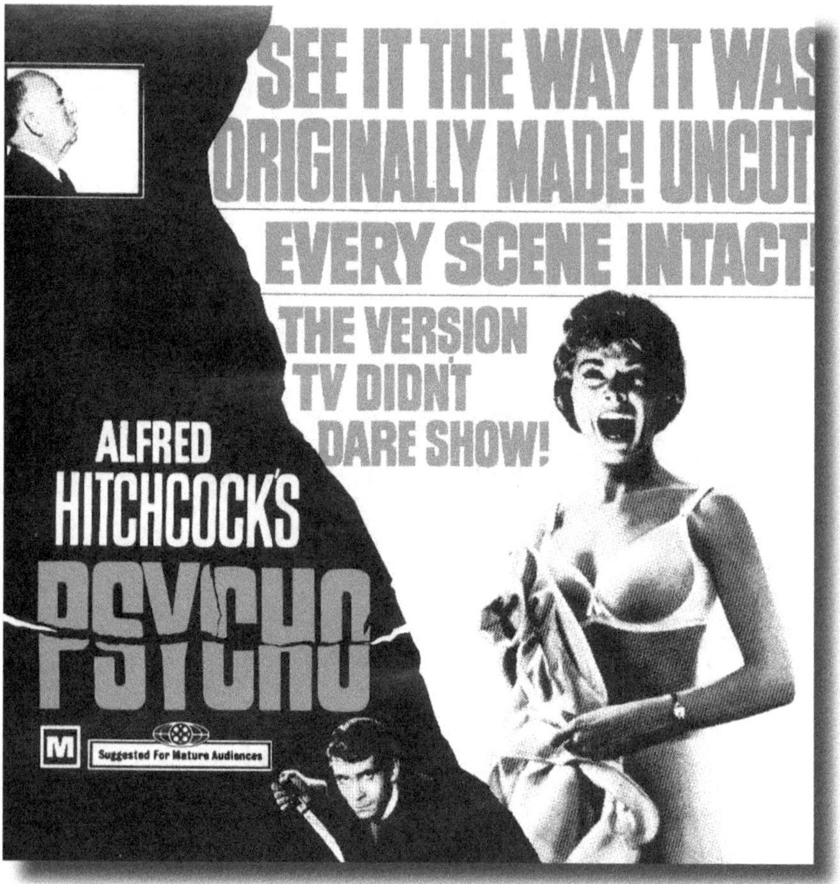

'Psycho' would be released in theaters numerous times after 1960 finding new audiences and bringing new profits to both Universal and the director. A poster (above) promoting one of the re-releases promised to show the version without cuts from a TV broadcast. Vera Miles (left) would reprise her role as Lila in the sequel some 20 years later. Miles had worked with Hitchcock numerous times, including appearances in 'The Wrong Man' and his TV series. She was at one time the intended star for 'Vertigo.'

Hitchcock on the set of his 1960 classic 'Psycho'.

Alfred Hitchcock enjoyed putting himself in the spotlight of his motion pictures rather than many of his stars. This became increasingly common during his iconic years of the 1960s and 1970s. Here he poses for a publicity shot..

THE LOST HITCHCOCKS

In her first major film role, Tippi Hedren was cast as the leading lady for Hitchcock's 1963 suspense horror film, 'The Birds', but the director and his thousands of feathered friends were the real stars of the picture.

Tippi Hedren was in nearly every scene of 'The Birds' and would follow it up with 'Marnie,' costarring Sean Connery. Hitchcock planned for her to appear in 'Mary Roes," but the film was never completed.

THE LOST HITCHCOCKS

Hitchcock and Universal knew they had a good shot at a hit with a follow-up film to 'Psycho,' but they provided theater owners with tips and instruction to capitalize on the promotional materials they provided them.

Hitchcock toyed with the media in his promotion of the film but promised to offer attacks from 'The Birds.'

Promotion of most of Hitchcock's projects in his later years, film, books, TV shows, magazines, albums and other , focused often on Hitchcock himselt.

Bodega Bay, north of San Francisco, provided the backdrop for much of the action in 'The Birds.' Above, the church and below, Tides Wharf Restaurant were real locations featured in key scenes.

THE LOST HITCHCOCKS

In addition to films, TV and paperback books Hitchcock even lent his name and image to a board game that capitalized on his brand of suspense and mystery.

THE LOST HITCHCOCKS

Hitchcock would be an icon by the release of his last few films. He was awarded a star on Hollywood's Walk of Fame in February 1960.

THE LOST HITCHCOCKS

With smiles all around, Alfred Hitchcock accompanied Tippi Hedren to the Cannes Film Festival to present his 1963 film 'The Birds.' Hedren, as the leading lady of the film would already be gearing up for her second Hitchcock film, 'Marnie,' in 1964. And while she was at one time planning even a third film with the director to follow 'Marnie,' a falling out with the director would cause him to cancel the film and end his association with Hedren.

Rod Taylor and Tippi Hedren were both relative newcomers to major motion pictures when Hitchcock cast them as lovers in 'The Birds.'

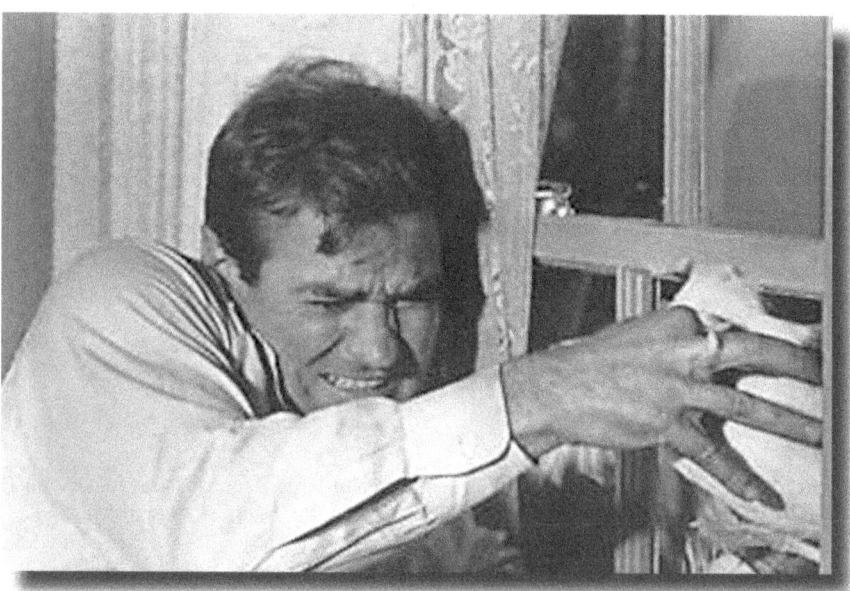

Rod Taylor fit the mold of the standard Hitchcock leading man. With rugged features like other Hitchcock actors, Cary Grant and John Gavin, Taylor's leading role in 'The Birds' had him acting as much with feathered co-stars as he did with human ones.

Hitchcock has long been a favorite of film magazines. In addition to his own magazines, Hitchcock has frequented many magazine covers as journalists continue to analyze and discuss his work and its impact on film.

Promotion for 'Marnie.'

Tippi Hedren and Sean Connery in a scene from 'Marnie.'

Hitchcock again used his own likeness to promote 'Torn Curtain' instead of its stars Paul Newman and Julie Andrews.

THE LOST HITCHCOCKS

Hitchcock's most famous film location, the Bates Motel and infamous home of Norman Bates held residence on the Universal lot for many years and was recreated in Florida at Universal Studios theme park. The various locations have been used over the years for several sequels, including 'Psycho II' and 'Psycho III' as well as the cable prequel 'Psycho IV.'

Hitchcock's TV series would end in the mid-1960s after nearly 10 years on the small screen, but it would make him one of the most recognizable faces and richest men in Hollywood.

Hitchcock would use his name and face to promote everything from films, TV shows, books, a fan magazine, board games and even music albums.

THE LOST HITCHCOCKS

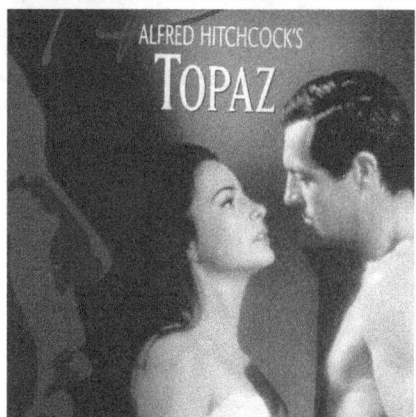
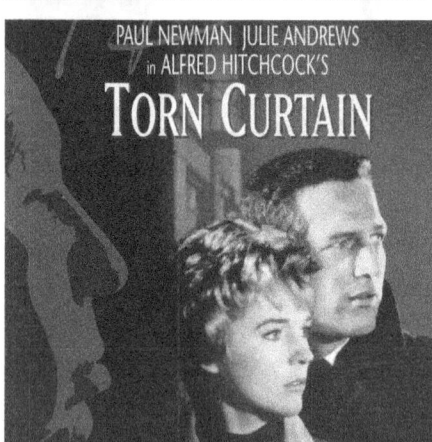

Universal DVD releases of Hitchcock's films continue find audiences as films are reissued with extra features and new digital transfers of the original films.

THE LOST HITCHCOCKS

Universal was wise to promote their association with Hitchcock and his long career in the film industry. His PR photos during his later years used his many successes and numerous films to remind viewers that Hitchcock's newest film 'Family Plot' would be the latest in the long line of suspense hits.

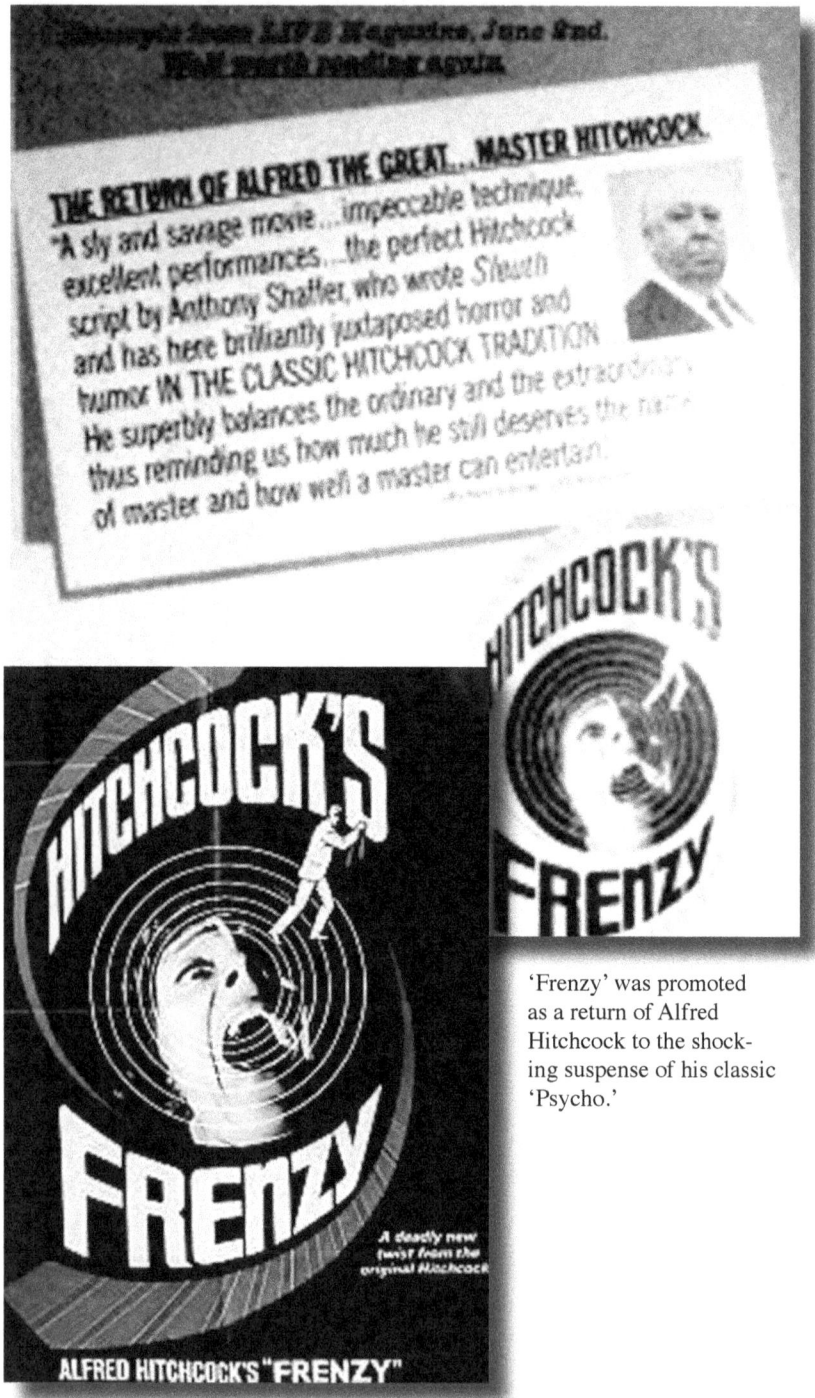

'Frenzy' was promoted as a return of Alfred Hitchcock to the shocking suspense of his classic 'Psycho.'

THE LOST HITCHCOCKS

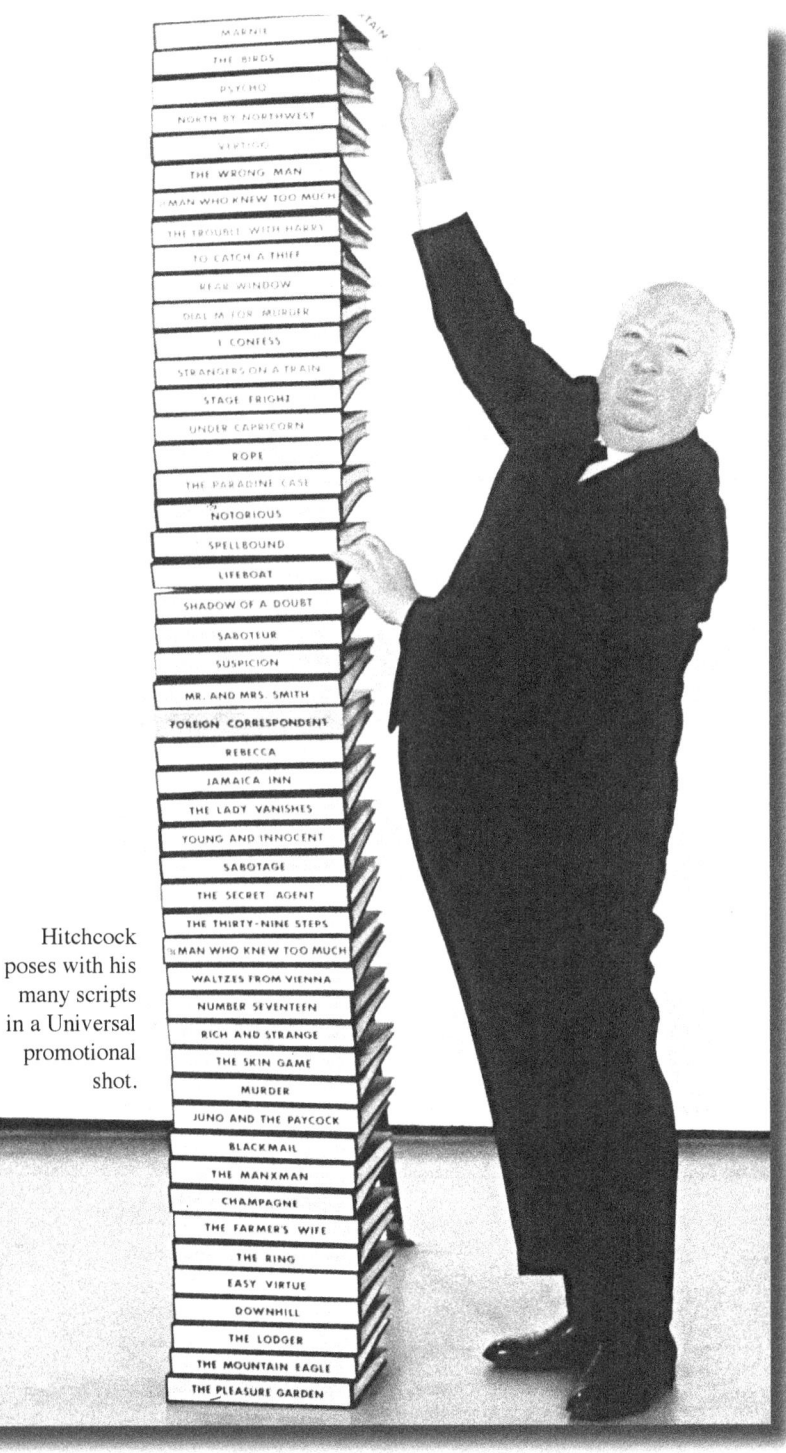

Hitchcock poses with his many scripts in a Universal promotional shot.

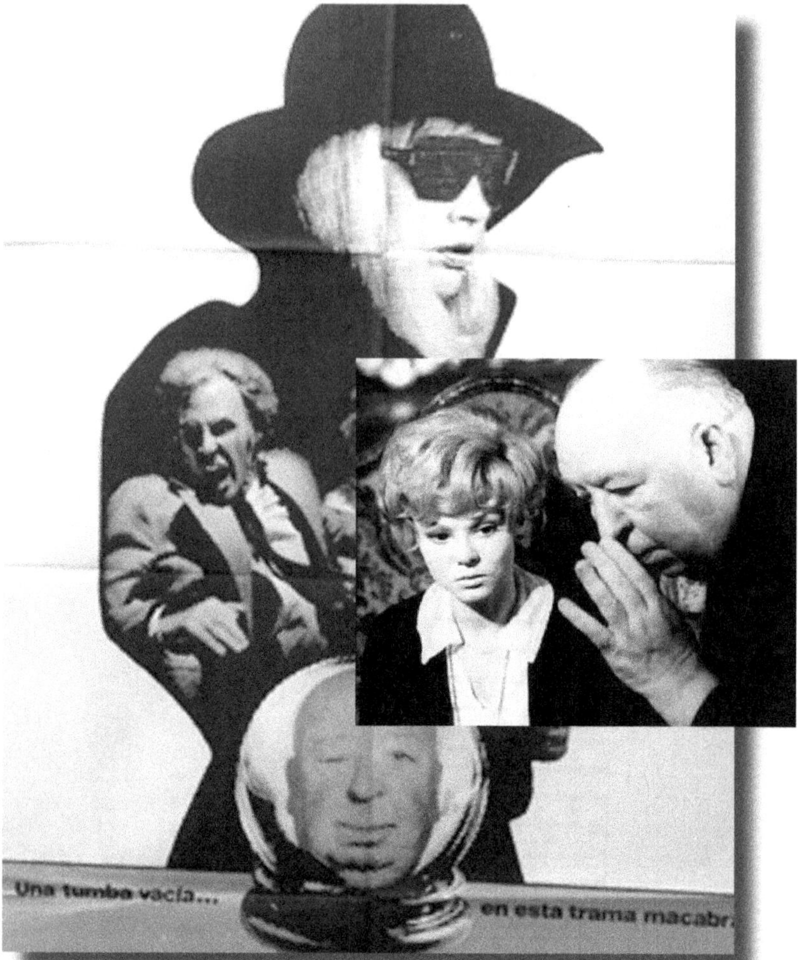

THE LOST HITCHCOCKS

Hitchcock, true to form, would again use himself as a marketing point to promote his final film, 'Family Plot' when it was released in March 1976.

THE LOST HITCHCOCKS

fourteen

THE LOST HITCHCOCKS

"Now, the reason I dropped the project is that I feel you cannot put hypnotism on the screen and expect it to hold water."

- Alfred Hitchcock

The Three Hostages

In the summer of 1964, when asked by the press what his next project would be, Alfred Hitchcock told reporters that his next film would be a return to his British roots. The film was intended to be an adaptation of John Buchan's novel, *The Three Hostages*. It was not the first time Buchan's work was the inspiration for a Hitchcock film.

Hitchcock struggled for years to bring *Greenmantle* to the big screen, and he also considered remaking *The 39 Steps* during his Hollywood years, after he had achieved success in Britain with the film, years earlier.

For this Buchan outing, the same lead character, Richard Hannay, is asked by British government officials to rescue three children who have been kidnapped and are being held hostage by a band of criminals. Locating and releasing the children, while putting a stop to other terrorist activities, is Hannay's dangerous mission.

THE LOST HITCHCOCKS

Robert Donat played Hannay in *The 39 Steps* and was considered one of the frontrunners if *Greenmantle* ever gotten off the ground. However, by 1964 Donat was no longer an option for the director. Donat suffered from chronic asthma, and as his career went on it became more of a limitation and liability. He would appear in only 20 films. In 1952, he was cast as Thomas Becket in T.S. Eliot's *Murder in the Cathedral* at the Old Vic Theatre. However, asthma attacks forced him to withdraw during the theatrical run. His final film role was the mandarin Yang Cheng in *The Inn of the Sixth Happiness* in 1958. He died on June 9, 1958 at the age of 53 in London. While it was suggested that his long battle with asthma was the cause of his death, it was discovered he actually had a brain tumor the size of an egg that caused a cerebral thrombosis, which was ultimately named the primary cause of his death.

Hitchcock had named no other possible successors to the role of Hannay in his pre-production plans for *The Three Hostages*, but rather spent his time focusing on getting the film's story in place. *The Three Hostages* was the fourth of five Hannay novels by Buchan and was first published in 1924 by London publisher, Hodder & Stoughton. *The Thirty Nine Steps*, published in 1915, first featured Hannay and was followed up with *Greenmantle* in 1916. The third Hannay novel was entitled *Mr. Standfast* and published in 1919.

For the film version of the fourth novel, Hitchcock hoped to rely on the novel's basic premise. Hannay would be on the trail of a group of Bolshevik criminals who have kidnapped three children from prominent British parents. The sinister criminal organization would be similar to *The Man Who Knew Too Much*, and little would need to be explained. The group simply came into power after the end of the war and uses hypnotism and mind control to cause terrorism. It is being tracked by police forces around the world. After the kidnapping each family receives a mysterious poem that links the kidnappings. Hannay uses references in the poems to piece together clues behind the crimes.

Hitch thought most movies portrayed the traditional spy, "speaking in guttural accents" as they "slink in and out of rooms." He felt his approach could be different. "True spies are not usually made in that mold. Ten to one, their English is perfect. Ten to one, they were born right next door. Ten to one, they play their real-life parts so well and so cleverly they never need to slink, nor look over their shoulders suspiciously. Some of them even – and you can keep an eye on your headlines to check this – are married to your best friend's best friend's friend. The connections of some of America's spies today are unimpeachable. It would appear to be insulting to question them."

However, Hitchcock had two major stumbling blocks in getting *The Three Hostages* to the big screen. First, his biggest challenge was his inability to secure the film rights to the story from Buchan's estate. This was the same challenge he faced in bringing *Greenmantle* to the screen, and would ultimately doom the film.

The second reason for abandoning the concept was because the story centered on hypnotism as a key plot element. Hitchcock didn't think the idea would work on screen. Although he had used hypnotism successfully in *Spellbound* in the 1940s, he wasn't sure 1960s audiences would believe the story. Hitchcock told writer and filmmaker Francois Truffaut that the hypnotism storyline didn't plausibly translate to the screen. Hitchcock described a scene from the novel where the villain uses his blind mother to hypnotize the hero in the film. Hitchcock had Universal's research department look into whether or not it was possible for a blind person to hypnotize someone. While theoretically possible, making it believable for modern movie audiences would be more difficult.

A third blow to the director would arrive near the end of 1964, closing the book on a film version of *The Three Hostages*. One of Hitchcock's most trusted partners, George Tomasini, died suddenly in November that year. A key player in Hitchcock's "creative team," Tomasini died of a sudden heart attack during a hunting trip with friends. A film editor, he edited many of Hitchcock's best-known films during the director's most productive years, including *Vertigo, Rear Window, Psycho* and *The Birds*. He was nominated for an Academy Award for Film Editing for

North by Northwest. Tomasini, along with associate producer Robert Burke, costume designer Edith Head, production assistant Joan Harrison and camera operator Leonard South, would make up Hitchcock's inner circle and creative team. Tomasini would have been a key member of the team to bring life to *The Three Hostages,* and his death was fatal blow to the project at this early stage.

Hitchcock was saddened of Tomasini's passing and would find it difficult to replace him. He would drop the idea for *The Three Hostages* before even finding a suitable writer. After a year of negotiations, Hitchcock's agents were still unable to come to agreement on a purchase price for the movie rights to *The Three Hostages* from Buchan's estate, so Hitch pulled the plug on the project.

The director would turn to the cold war for his next film instead. Starring two of Hollywood's biggest stars at the time, Julie Andrews and Paul Newman, *Torn Curtain* would be Hitchcock's actual completed film in place of *The Three Hostages*.

THE LOST HITCHCOCKS

fifteen

THE LOST HITCHCOCKS

"The need for profit is just as valid today as it was in the past. Even if I wanted to make, write, play, and finance a film on my own, I couldn't do it because I would run into problems with the trade unions."

- Alfred Hitchcock

Kaleidoscope

After Hitchcock completed *Torn Curtain* in the spring of 1966, he turned his attention to the task of finalizing the promotion of his latest film and the host of media activities required for getting a movie in front of audiences. While part of Hitchcock certainly hated the task of "selling" a movie, there was a part of him driven by the attention that accompanied each release and his chance to be in the spotlight. For Hitchcock, it was a delicate balance he would walk his entire career.

He sometimes said that once a film was completed in his head, and he worked through the storyboards and technically achieved the concept, he'd lose interest in the actual casting, costumes, set design and filming of the story. He could easily be bored by the camera work and performers, or frustrated when scripts were incomplete, as production got underway.

Stars sometimes complained that Hitchcock failed to provide them with useful direction or motivation for their characters. His main concern was to capture the actions and the angles he so desired and as long as the actors got their lines right, and moved on cue to the rhythm he had demanded of them, he was satisfied. While some actors invited the freedom this provided, others struggled with it.

Actors like Gary Grant, Ingrid Bergman, Jimmy Stewart, and Janet Leigh found working with Hitchcock a pleasure because they had the ability to define the internal make-up of the character and understood the constraints of what Hitchcock expected of them. While other actors, including his most recent experience with Paul Newman and Julie Andrews, seemed to require more dialogue and understanding of what they were expected to deliver and wanted more than a cue of where to walk or how to look.

While Hitchcock bored of much of the filmmaking process that followed his screenplay, he adored the attention moviemaking offered him. For a portly, older fellow, he longed for attention and found that being the "star" director had its pluses, because he would be sought after and treated as a celebrity.

In fact, his TV series, *Alfred Hitchcock Presents*, turned him into more than just a household name – he had already been that – but by the sixties he was one of the most recognizable faces in Hollywood. His desire for attention and acclaim was fueled by the release of each film. It gave him and opportunity to film TV spots, movie promotions, and plan advertising campaigns that centered on his likeness.

He gave interviews to TV, magazines and newspapers and loved the acclaim that came with each release. However, if his movie suffered in the hands of critics he could be depressed by the disappointing reception, only to cover it up with disdain for the reviewers.

Before *Torn Curtain* could garner such reviews, Hitch accepted an invitation to deliver an address at Cambridge. He accepted it for several reasons. First, it was a chance to head back to England. He always enjoyed traveling back to his homeland and any trip where he could tie it to his work was a welcome one. Second, he once again loved the notoriety of being sought after as a speaker. For others to want to hear what he had to say was what drove him to do what he did. So, in June 1966, he flew to the United Kingdom to address to the Cambridge University Film Society. The event offered both a chance for Hitchcock to deliver an address, and then take part in a discussion period with the students about his work. When asked about the future of film he told the audience, "Mass hypnotism would be a nice idea for the future. You buy a ticket and choose the character you want to be," said Hitchcock. "If you want to be the villain, then you have a good time being the villain. If you want to be the tortured victim, you can suffer."

Hitch then continued to bask in the glory of his long and successful career by accepting New York City's Cultural Medal of Honor in July. He flew from London to New York for a ceremony at City Hall where the honor was bestowed upon him. He also gave a series of media interviews and the event provided him an opportunity to also tout his upcoming release before the reviews would come in.

His summer of adulation continued when he headed to Massachusetts to accept an honor from then Governor John Volpe when the governor declared July 14, 1966 as "Alfred Hitchcock Day" across the Commonwealth of Massachusetts. Then it was off to Boston University for another special citation for his career accomplishments. To top things off, Harvard University also gave him an honorary membership to the Harvard Drama Club that month.

Also in July, Hitchcock was invited to Toronto to address the students of the University of Toronto, on "The Art and Business of Filmmaking." He also spoke to The Directors Guild of Canada and then it was back to London where he was honored with an award from the Association of Cinematograph, Television and Allied Technicians. He then attended a luncheon in London that August where the London Film

Alfred Hitchcock by the late 1960s was a seasoned filmmaker, but looked to stay current in the industry

Society forgave Hitchcock for abandoning the United Kingdom and the world of European filmmaking world for the bright lights of Hollywood. The association then hosted a dinner where Hitchcock was awarded an honorary membership. Hitchcock returned to his Los Angeles home at the end of the summer and even though the reviews of his latest work were less than enthusiastic he was warmed by the acclaim he had earned from his complete body of work, and one film wouldn't detract from all that he had accomplished.

Then, in 1967, the Academy of Motion Picture Arts and Sciences would honor Hitchcock at their annual Academy Awards ceremony with the coveted Irving Thalberg award for his contribution to cinema. Although never presenting him with the coveted Oscar for directing, the academy presented him with the award saying, "When you examine the list of his films you are jolted by the legion of absolutely top level entertainment he has made – a record almost unmatched by any director practicing his magic anywhere ... a body of work so distinctive that his name has passed into the language ... his briefly titled masterpieces of suspense, adventure and humor have endeared him to film buffs as certainly as his own fey presence on the small screen has endeared him to television audiences."

By the end of August, fellow filmmaker Francois Truffaut welcomed Hitchcock for a series of interviews. In fact, in one of the most detailed efforts chronicling Hitchcock's views, Truffaut recorded more than 50 hours of discussion between himself and the master of suspense as Hitchcock discussed his films, actors and career in great length and much detail, including his current feature.

Overall, *Torn Curtain* in some ways was a throwback to Hitchcock's traditional filmmaking process. Shooting on a soundstage allowed him the control he desired, but filmmaking was taking a step forward and younger filmmakers were taking risks that put them outside the traditions and their work was being noticed for it. Hitchcock's work became visibly more dated and his approach would require updating. In fact, several of the scenes in *Torn Curtain* capture scenes reminiscent of his previous work. The opening sequence features a soft-focus close-up kiss that was similar to shots Hitch included successfully in both *Rear Window* and *Marnie*. The farmhouse sequence offers a very similar feel to *North By Northwest* when Cary Grant is walking across the open field just prior to the crop-duster scenes. It features a "danger comes in the most ordinary places" approach.

Hitchcock would rebound from *Torn Curtain*. The film was by no means a colossal failure, but it was a project that never lived up to the expectations anyone had for it. Many times, as Hitchcock reached stumbling blocks he would abandon a film and move onto the next project. In some ways that might have been the case with *Torn Curtain* had so much money not been invested or the two leading box office stars of the day not been attached to the picture. The profits came in and the critics were not nearly as harsh on the film as they were on several other Hitchcock pictures.

While Hitchcock would take a break from filmmaking and Hollywood in 1967 he would return to the world he loved in 1968 with a new project and another attempt to once again wow the critics. He had become impressed with the work of Italian director, screenwriter, and editor Michelangelo Antonioni. *Blow Up* was an international smash in 1966, and put Antonioni on the map as a director of note. Hitchcock wanted to achieve the same frankness and sexuality, while still trying to be true to the Hitchcock classic. It was an idea to stay current with filmmaking, but remain faithful to the audience.

The idea for his next film was actually something of a twist on the *Psycho* concept. Hitchcock wanted to do Hollywood's take on Neville Heath, a killer known as the Baby-Faced Killer. Heath was found guilty and hanged for the gruesome murders of two young women in the summer of 1946. The women had been bound, stabbed, beaten and the crime had shaken many for the brutal nature of the killings. Hitchcock was drawn to the nature of the crime and the killer, a handsome, yet perverted psychopath.

To recapture the success of *Psycho*, Peggy Robertson, Hitchcock's assistant, was instructed to convince *Psycho* author, Robert Bloch, to agree to write an original story that would eventually become *Kaleidoscope*. The two reportedly agreed to terms, with Hitchcock registering the original idea with the Writers Guild on November 9, 1964. The concept noted that murders by John George Haigh and Neville Heath were part of the inspiration for the fictional story.

When Bloch bowed out of the project, reportedly because he "found the characters too disturbing," Hitchcock asked an old friend, Benn Levy, to help him flesh out a first draft of the screenplay. Hitchcock had worked with Levy in 1932, producing his film, *Lord Camber's Ladies*, and although history suggests the collaboration did not end on the most positive of terms, the two men kept in touch and in early 1966 embarked on crafting the story for *Kaleidoscope*, sometimes referred to as *Frenzy*. While *Frenzy* would be realized in the early 1970s, the script and story differ from *Kaleidoscope* and Hitchcock mainly used the suggested title for the earlier work for his later work.

Levy flew from London to New York in early 1966 to meet Hitchcock and the two men went on a tour along the edge of the Hudson River, scouting out locations for the film, including a waterfall and some mothballed ships. In the initial treatment Hitchcock and Levy came up with three murders – one taking place by the waterfall, a second occurring in an abandon old ship, and the third during the climax of the picture, at an oil refinery with oil tanks painted in primary colors.

During the summer of 1967 Hitchcock reworked Levy's initial treatment, fleshing out the story further, but he had trouble bringing the story to life. Some suggest that Hitchcock's treatment took Levy's concept further, but was still, "as close to the bone as possible," and that the third and final act suffered from "weaknesses."

Writers Howard Fast and Hugh Wheeler were brought in to draft a filmable screenplay, but Hitchcock had formed no bond with the writers. In fact, one factor in the struggle to bring *Kaleidoscope* to the big screen was another death of a longtime Hitchcock partner, Robert Burkes. Burkes, like George Tomasini, was a core member of the director's creative team. He began his career as a special effects technician in the late 1930s, but would find his greatest success as a director of photography and cinematography. While he worked on a number of other features, starting in the 1940s, his work with Hitchcock put him on the map, beginning with *Strangers on a Train* in 1951. He followed Hitchcock after that with work on I *Confess, Dial M For Murder, Rear Window, The Trouble With Harry, The Man Who Knew Too Much, The Wrong Man, Vertigo, North by Northwest, The Birds,* and *Marnie*. He was nominated for an Oscar for his work on *Strangers on a Train*, but wouldn't win the coveted statue until 1955 for *To Catch a Thief.*

Burks and his wife died in a house fire in Huntington Harbor, California, in May 1968. The cinematographer reportedly nodded off while smoking a cigarette in bed, setting the house on fire. Hitchcock was shocked and saddened to learn of the death of his old friend.

Hitchcock was drawn to the darkness of the *Kaleidoscope* story, but also the sexuality, and in notes he discussed the specific details of the murder of one of the leading ladies. "Actually we can mark the body with streaks but never go close on them. His pants are on. His fingers are on her throat. He goes downstairs, picks up his coat and puts it on. I suppose we don't dare have him put her clothes on her body? He doesn't care about covering her identity."

Hitchcock wanted to take *Kaleidoscope* much further than he had taken *Psycho*. In fact, he knew film was evolving into a far more gritty and real experience than it was when he'd made *Psycho* at the turn of the decade. Camera and sound equipment had grown far more portable and location shooting was becoming the norm, as opposed to soundstages. In fact, one of the criticisms labeled on some of Hitchcock's more recent films, like *Marnie* and *Torn Curtain,* was his dependence on Hollywood tricks like films on soundstages and rear projections tactics.

For *Kaleidoscope*, Hitchcock intended to look to more innovative and newer filming techniques, like handheld camera equipment, point-of-view shooting, and the use of natural light. It would also feature more nudity than the director had ever been able to present on the big screen. Hitch went so far as to fly to New York to scout locations for the film and use new camera equipment to tape four reels of film that equated to roughly 40 minutes of footage, using unknown actors in natural light and real settings. The silent footage represents the only footage ever captured for the possible film and mostly focused on different lighting settings and techniques using various film stocks.

One scene featured a young female model getting up from her bed in a New York apartment. The model was nude and filmed using natural light, as she gets up and walk to the bathroom. Another scene at an art studio shows another nude model, this time encountering the killer. Hitchcock reportedly told Arthur Schatz, a still photographer he used to photograph possible locations, that he intended to film a young actor masturbating in bed, only to be caught by his mother.

"Basically, he wanted a lot of shots of various New York City locations with actors. He gave me total freedom as to how to do it," Schatz recalled. "I remember riding around the city with him – Hitchcock in the front passenger seat (I was sitting in the back) – and as we reached the locations, he would tell me the story of what was happening in the film. He really was a great man to work with."

Schatz recalled that after he produced the shots, he flew out to Los Angeles and met with Hitchcock in a screening room to review them. "He loved the work. He was very complimentary and seemed very excited about the project," he recalled.

Hitchcock was excited by the potential the film held, after he completed the initial film work in July 1967. Unfortunately, Hitchcock's enthusiasm would not be shared by Universal. They rejected the idea outright.

By this stage, his agent, Lew Wasserman, held greater control over Hitchcock's Universal films, focusing on "corporate-packaged" films where the director, story, and stars were aligned under the Universal banner in hopes of driving more profit. Hitchcock resisted, knowing the industry was changing and recognized that to stay contemporary, he had to push the envelope. A new wave of modern French films, as well as contemporary Italian cinema, provided ideas Hitchcock very much wanted to pursue. However, the director had to walk a fine line in finding ways to incorporate the brutal realism and modern day film concepts into studio projects that promised a more traditional Universal hit film. Because the European films of the day offered more graphic violence and nudity, Hitchcock looked for ways to introduce more rawness into his feature film projects.

While it is true that by the late 1960s Hitchcock was a wealthy man and could have independently funded the production of a film without studio backing. However, Hitchcock's relationship with Universal limited his ability to go it alone, and with recent box office misses, a failure might have ended his relationship and limited his ability to keep working. At his age, Hitchcock wasn't the man he was a decade earlier and avoided difficult situations that could have had costly consequences.

Wasserman would ultimately be one of the key architects behind the refusal to allow Hitchcock to craft *Kaleidoscope,* forcing him down a more traditional route with *Topaz.* Hitchcock's lack of enthusiasm for the Leon Uris novel, coupled with his disappointment over not being able to make the film he really desired to make, would spell doom for *Topaz.*

In fact, a number of those closest to the director were not enthusiastic about the idea. François Truffaut, director and writer, as well as Hitchcock confidant was given a chance to read an early version of the script. He reportedly felt uncomfortable at the "aggressive themes of sex and violence." Truffaut felt that while *Psycho* "blended those themes with the narrative of a mystery and psychological suspense," in *Kaleidoscope*, the murderer would be difficult to accept as the main star of the film and that audiences would find it difficult to accept him and root for him, certainly if he was an unknown actor. By avoiding expensive sets and special effects, and using a cast of unknown actors, Hitchcock felt the low cost production would easily help the studio recoup its cost, but Universal said no.

Hitchcock was crushed by the studio dismissal. He felt he was a proven hit maker and commodity for the studio and wasn't used to being told no. However, in reality his last few films had performed less than expected and was easier not giving into Hitchcock's whims. *Topaz, Torn Curtain* and *Marnie* all failed to meet studio expectations. While *The Birds* had done well, it was in part the excitement at the director's follow up film to *Psycho*. *Psycho* had not even been made for Universal, even though the studio acquired rights to the film.

    Hitchcock would manage to lift some elements of *Kaleidoscope* for his 1972 film *Frenzy*, and see some realization of a work he put so much time and energy into. The rare silent footage of *Kaleidoscope* might have been lost, except for the fact that Hitchcock held onto it personally. After Alma Hitchcock's death in 1982 the film was discovered in the Hitchcock home and donated to the Margaret Herrick Library of the Academy of Motion Picture Arts and Sciences.

THE LOST HITCHCOCKS

sixteen

THE LOST HITCHCOCKS

"A novel may lose a lot of its interest in the translated version, and a play that's beautifully acted out on opening night may become shapeless during the rest of the run, but a film travels all over the world. Assuming that it loses fifteen percent of its impact when it's subtitled and ten percent when it's well dubbed, the image remains intact, even when the projection is faulty. It's your work that's being shown – nothing can alter that – and you're expressing yourself in the same terms everywhere."

- Alfred Hitchcock

Jaws

It probably comes as no surprise that Steven Spielberg considered Alfred Hitchcock one of his greatest heroes. Growing up with his suspense films was one of the inspirations that drove him to a life and career in film. However, Spielberg never got the chance to meet Hitchcock personally. Hitchcock refused. Spielberg is said to consider not meeting Hitchcock one of the biggest disappointments of his life.

'Jaws,' the novel by Peter Benchley was a bestseller.

THE LOST HITCHCOCKS

It certainly wasn't because Spielberg didn't try. In fact, according to *Tales of Hollywood*, by Stephen Schochet, during the making of Hitchcock's last completed film, *Family Plot*, the Master of Suspense was, "upset by an uninvited young man hovering around the movie set," one morning in 1975. The story goes that the aging director called upon a crew member to "have the trespasser removed," and that the intruder was Spielberg, there in hopes of meeting his idol.

That was simply one instance. Other reports suggest that during the last years of his life, Hitchcock refused to meet Spielberg on numerous occasions. Especially after the young director's newfound success, following *Jaws*. His reluctance was a mystery until actor Bruce Dern, explained why in his autobiography. Dern appeared in two Hitchcock films, *Marnie* and *Family Plot,* and it was during the completion of the latter that Dern learned why.

Dern says that he tried to convince Hitchcock to introduce himself to Spielberg: "I said, 'You're his idol. He just [wants] to sit at your feet for five minutes and chat with you,' but Hitchcock refused," Dern wrote.

"He said, 'Isn't that the boy who made the fish movie?... I could never sit down and talk to him ... because I look at him and feel like such a whore.'"

A confused Dern asked Hitchcock to explain why. "I said, 'Why do you feel Spielberg makes you a whore?'"

Hitch responded, "Because I'm the voice of the *Jaws* ride [at the Universal Studios theme park]. They paid me a million dollars. And I took it and I did it. I'm such a whore. I can't sit down and talk to the boy who did the fish movie ... I couldn't even touch his hand.'"

What Hitchcock didn't admit, was that he too had considered making *Jaws.* Had he accepted the film, a young Steven Spielberg might not have made his breakthrough film.

Back in 1973, Hitchcock was celebrating the success of his most recent film, *Frenzy*, and was contemplating what might come next. He was also honored with a glowing retrospective of his work in January

1973 when the Los Angeles County Museum of Modern Art, in cooperation with the American Film Institute, offered, "Presenting Alfred Hitchcock," an exhibition of 21 of Hitchcock's classic features. Starting with *Rear Window* and ending roughly a month later with his latest film *Frenzy*, it would also include nine of the episodes he directed of his decade long television series.

Then in March that year he was again honored, this time by the International Alliance of Theatrical Stage Employees who presented him with an award for Motion Picture Showmanship, during a luncheon in Hollywood. As the year progressed Hitch spent much of his free time reading books and looking for possible film projects.

Two projects that came his way were based on novels. One was by English author Victor Canning and was called *The Rainbird Pattern*. The other, a suspenseful horror by Peter Benchley called *Jaws*.

The *The Rainbird Pattern* was comfortable ground for the director as it had all the standard elements audiences might expect from a Hitchcock thriller, though it lacked some of the more gruesomeness visuals of more recent hits like *The Birds* and *Psycho*. The original title, *The Rainbird Pattern*, was abandoned for the film, however, when it was first changed to *One Plus One Equals One* when the project was announced to the media in late 1973 as Hitchcock's next picture.

Jaws, on the other hand, had the gore *The Rainbird Pattern* lacked. The screenplay was based on a yet unpublished book by Benchley and landed at Universal in 1973. Benchley began writing the book in the mid-60s after reading about a Long Island shark fisherman who had harpooned a shark weighing roughly 4,500 pounds. It would be published in February 1973 and quickly became a best seller.

Spielberg claimed he "stole" the galley proofs off the desk of Richard Zanzuck, one of the heads of Universal. He saw it as the perfect opportunity to show his talents and wanted to direct the feature, but Spielberg was not what the studio initially had in mind.

The project was actually first turned down by ABC, after the network considered it for a TV movie. Network executives passed on the deal because they feared it would cost too much to produce. However, after the success of the hardback release of the book, a battle began for the paperback rights. Bantam came out on top after reportedly offering $575,000, and soon after, the idea of a feature film became a reality. If the book could create a stir, a movie could do more.

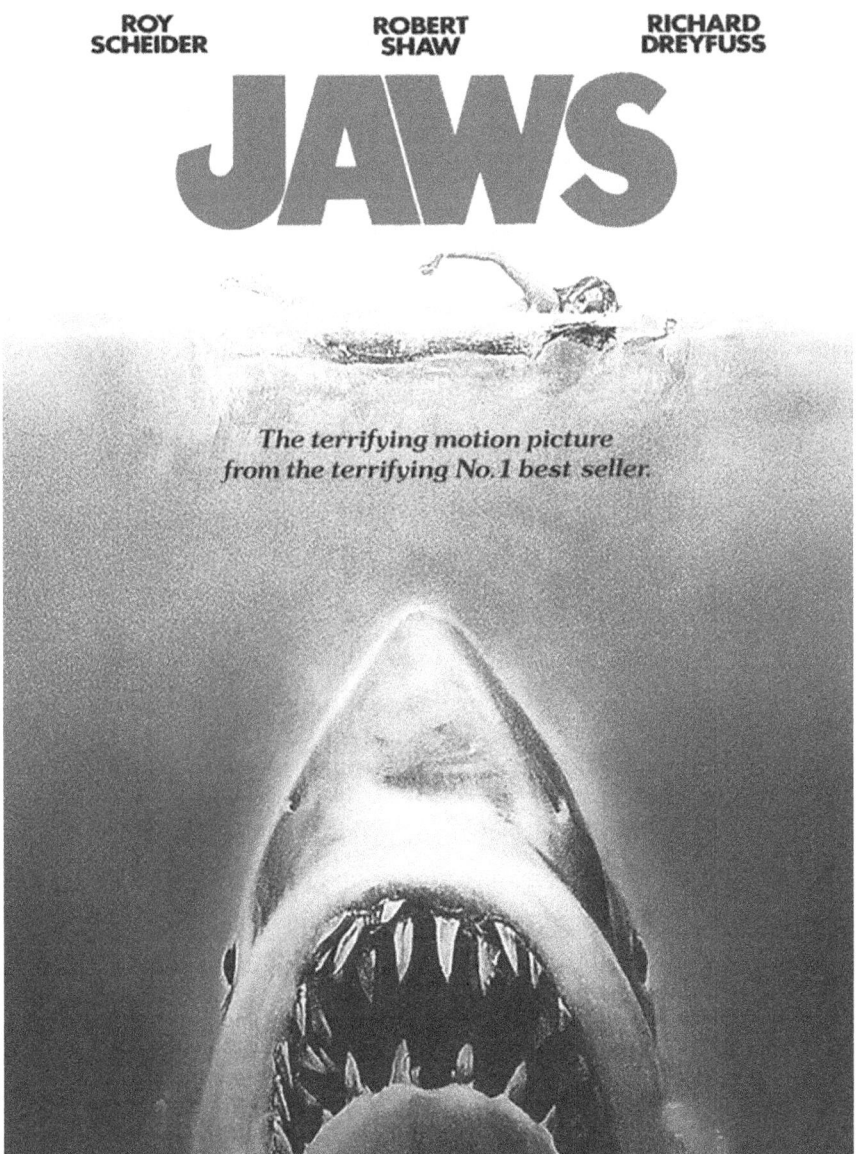

The film looked to cash in on the success of the novel.

THE LOST HITCHCOCKS

Once Universal executives caught wind of the book they saw a hit movie and the book began making its rounds. Getting name talent and a skilled director would get the film made. Paul Newman was one of the first actors the studio had in mind for the project. For the role of director, Hitchcock was Universal's first choice.

Hitchcock arrived at Universal around 1961 after the release of *Psycho*. *The Birds* would be his first film under the terms of his new contract, and nearly every suspense screenplay or horror script that came through the studio gates afterwards, was presented to Hitchcock for consideration, or he was given the right of first refusal.

The film rights to *Jaws* were obtained and Universal began initial plans of making the feature for a mere $750,000. Some were skeptical that the movie could be made on such a low budget. Filming on water is often the most difficult of locations, but the studio heads believed it could be managed on less than a million dollars. They would be wrong.

Hitchcock had worked with Paul Newman before. The two men collaborated on *Torn Curtain* in the mid-1960s, but the effort failed to ignite moviegoers and the experience was not a pleasant one for either man. With Newman's method acting interfering with Hitchcock's style, the two butted heads on numerous occasions. It was unlikely either Hitchcock or Newman would want to revisit the experience. Hitchcock also had some experience working on water. While several of his films featured critical water scenes, like *Foreign Correspondent* and *The Birds*, his 1944 film *Lifeboat,* was filmed entirely in a confined space on the water, making it a technical challenge for the director.

Hitchcock, like many directors, found filming on water a difficult experience, the bouncing of light, winds, currents and quickly changing weather conditions proved to be nearly impossible to plan for, even when using a studio water tank – open seas were far more difficult. In his later years, Hitchcock's ability to sustain a challenging location shoot on water would have been difficult at best. He often preferred soundstages where he could control the conditions. *Jaws* meant putting himself up against a set of technical challenges that were outside his control, and it was a space he was reluctant to delve into at this stage of his life and career.

Hitchcock refused to consider *Jaws* seriously and Universal was left to look to other options for a director. John Sturges and Dick Richards were considered for the director spot, but when Spielberg expressed interest the studio eventually took notice. They wanted a film that would really shake up audiences. Universal felt a young director might be able to provide that, and they were impressed enough with his earlier works in TV to believe he could accomplish the task.

For casting, Spielberg wanted little known actors, so a celebrity like Paul Newman would cast a shadow over the film. "I wanted somewhat anonymous actors to be in it so you would believe this was happening to you and me," admitted the director. Richard Dreyfuss and Roy Scheider were cast in two of the male leads, and Robert Shaw, who had recently starred in *The Sting*, was a well-known actor, but not a star. The director won out, possibly because it would help keep the budget down.

Some have described *Jaw*s as, "the most difficult film ever made." When principle photography began in May 1974 the shooting schedule was set at 55 days. Things began on a bad note when the mechanical shark built to be the star of the film failed to work properly and as time went on things only got worse. The budget began to spiral out of control and the shooting schedule stretched.

As predicted, one of the biggest problems was shooting at sea. Most water features use tanks to shoot key scenes and close-ups so that they have more control over the surroundings. But Spielberg and the producers of the film wanted it filmed at sea so it would look authentic. It presented them with major difficulties and was one of the main reasons the schedule expanded as much as it did. In May 1974 *Jaws* began filming, Its planned 55-day shoot stretched into a 159-day shoot, and its initial $3.5 million budget topped $10 million. Hitchcock was right, but Spielberg had landed with a hit.

Universal opened the film in 400 theaters on June 20, 1975, and soon it was the number one movie across the country. The massive opening was a new idea to the studios and soon became commonplace. The film earned $129 million and soon everyone was afraid of the water. The summer of 1975 was a box office blast. It was the *Psycho* of 1975.

Hitchcock, on the other hand, decided to proceed with *The Rainbird Pattern*, but when production began 1975, the title had changed to something more similar to *Jaws* – a one-word title – "Deceit."

Hitchcock held a press luncheon to kick off the production, inviting the media to a cemetery set on the Universal lot, complete with miniature headstone placecards for the journalists in attendance. The film production would mark Hitchcock's 50th anniversary as a director and his 53rd feature film. Released nearly a year after *Jaws*, it would ultimately become the Master of Suspense's final completed film, retitled yet again as *Family Plot*. At a cost of about $4.5 million, the film would take in roughly $13.2 million.

seventeen

THE LOST HITCHCOCKS

"The main objective is to arouse the audience's emotion, and that emotion arises in the way in which the story unfolds, from the way in which sequences are juxtaposed. At times I have the feeling I am an orchestra conductor, a trumpet sound corresponding to a close shot and a distant shot suggesting an entire orchestra performing a muted accompaniment."

- Alfred Hitchcock

The Short Night

After *Family Plot*, Hitchcock was still a viable commodity and a filmmaker with clout in Hollywood. In fact, at a cost of roughly $4.5 million and a box office draw of more than $13.2 million in the United States alone, the success would enable Hitchcock to continue to develop projects as long as he was physically able.

As a filmmaker Hitchcock was always working on an idea. Some suggested Hitchcock could be like a shark, and that to stay alive he had to keep moving with a film project in play. As he aged and his health deteriorated, those closest to him knew it would kill him if he found himself unable to work.

Even during the off years, when a film wasn't in some stage of development, as an avid reader Hitch was continually look at new or even old novels for ideas of potential films. For many years he frequented the theater and kept and eye on the competition, in both the U.S. and Europe, to see what others were doing and look for inspiration from any source. Even the newspaper headlines proved useful for projects like *Psycho* and *The Birds*.

However, as detailed here, not all of Hitchcock's ideas or projects came to fruition as a finished product. Some of his film ideas, like *No Bail for the Judge, The Wreck of the Mary Deare, The Blind Man,* and *Mary Rose* worked their way through the process, but were blocked from completion for one reason or another. However, Hitchcock always had another project in the wings to focus on.

Hitchcock's last unfinished film to conclude his Universal contract was intended to be based on a spy novel by Ronald Kirkbride entitled *The Short Night*. It was an espionage thriller that Hitchcock had crafted into a screenplay with the idea of it being his follow-up feature to *Family Plot*. Based loosely on the true story of a British double agent named George Blake, the tale follows his escape from prison as he flees to Finland with plans to eventually reach Moscow. He expects to meet up with his wife and children who are waiting for him. In the meantime, an American agent, whose brother was one of the double agent's victims, is on his trail and arrives in Finland, hoping to intercept him. However, the agent ends up falling in love with the wife of the traitor and complications arise through a series of unexpected twists and turns.

Cut from the cloth of *Torn Curtain* and *Topaz*, the film represented a chance for Hitchcock to "get it right" at last, and produce a first-rate espionage suspense thriller. Potential leading men who were being considered for the leading male roles included Clint Eastwood, Walter Matthau, and Sean Connery, while Liv Ullman was reportedly approached about playing the double agent's wife.

The first writer assigned to the picture didn't see eye to eye with the director/producer and bowed out early on, so Hitchcock once again turned to Ernest Lehman, the writer who had helped bail Hitchcock out numerous times before on difficult projects. Even after Hitch swore never to work with Lehman, again after he dropped out of *The Blind Man* in

Sean Connery was proposed as the star for 'The Short Night." The photo is a mock up of a possible promotion for the incomplete film.

the early 1960s. So few of Hitch's inner circle were left that he found himself turning to familiar faces, even if disappointment lingered in his memory. Lehman, however, felt the story's focus should come from the perspective of the American agent and Hitchcock disagreed. So Hitchcock, disappointed once again, turned to another old friend, Norman Lloyd, who he had worked with on *Saboteur* many years before.

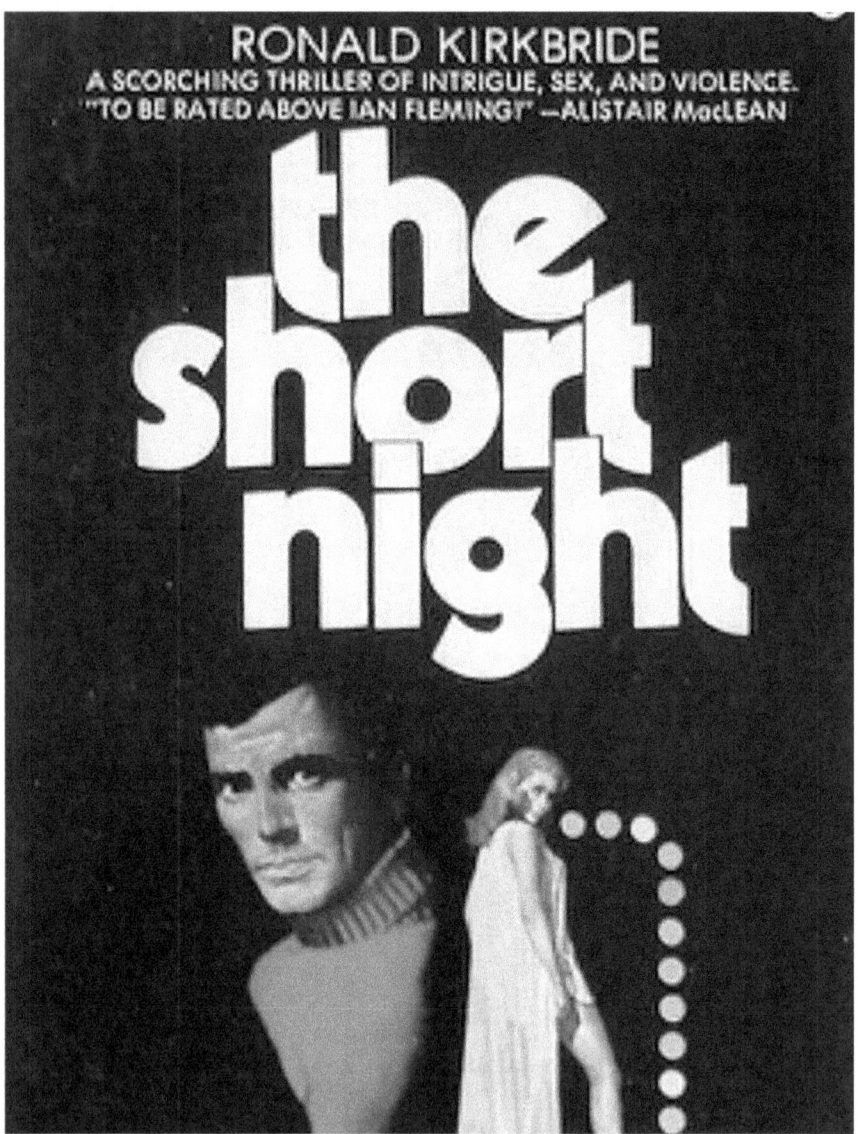

The novel on which the film was to be based.

Hitchcock wanted to quickly draft the screenplay before all the elements of the story were worked out. When Lloyd objected, Hitchcock decided to do the screenplay himself and reportedly fired Lloyd in a fit of anger.

Universal was a bit concerned that Hitchcock's failing health and advanced years would prevent the film from ever being made and was unsure he was up to the task. Hitchcock eventually agreed that he needed the help of a qualified writer and accepted Universal's offer of using David Freeman. Freeman helped Hitchcock iron out the story and produce a screenplay. A final draft was submitted and approved by the director in the fall of 1978 and it was this draft Hitchcock had Freeman modify.

However, during pre-production for the film in 1979, Hitchcock realized that his declining health would make directing the film impossible, so he asked old friend Hilton Green break the news to Universal that he had decided to retire.

Hitchcock would close the book on *The Short Night* and would never complete another film. Hitchcock would reluctantly retire as he realized his health was deteriorating and he no longer had the stamina to endure a lengthy development and production schedule. He also didn't have the strength to scout or film on the lengthy location shoots his films often required, nor could be deal with actors and crew as effectively as he had in the past. His contract with Universal still left him with one film to deliver, but Hitchcock realized he would never fulfill his contractual agreement with Universal. The studio also knew there was little they could do as the director was nearing the end of his life.

THE LOST HITCHCOCKS

eighteen

THE LOST HITCHCOCKS

"Because cinema is the greatest known mass medium there is in the world and the most powerful – if you've designed a picture correctly, in terms of its emotional impact, the Japanese audience should scream at the same time as the Indian audience. To a filmmaker, this is always the challenge."

- Alfred Hitchcock

The Death of Alfred Hitchcock

In his later years, Hitchcock became grounded to home at 10957 Bellagio Road in Bel Air. He'd purchased the home in the spring of 1942, after having spent his first few years in Hollywood, renting a smaller home, also in Bel-Air, owned by Carole Lombard. After Lombard's death in a plane crash in early 1942, the Hitchcock's needed to find a place of their own. While he once claimed all he needed was "a snug little house with a kitchen, and the devil with a swimming pool," his only Hollywood home was a bit grander. Hidden on a .64-acre lot, the Colonial style home held seven bedrooms, five baths and backed up against the Bel-Air Country Club. Hitch purchased the home for $40,000 and presented it to his wife for her birthday, hiding a gold key to the front door in a new handbag.

They owned a second home in Santa Cruz, Hitchcock had purchased in 1940 after filming *Rebecca*, where the family would often vacation. However, after the house was burglarized in 1970, Hitch sold the house and traveled less. As he grew older the Bellagio Road home became a sanctuary and safe haven. By late 1979 he seldom left.

Hitchcock had been in failing health during the last year of his life. At 80, he was still severely overweight, and his size, combined with arthritis and general complications that come with being a man of his age, made living difficult. In addition to the physical pain of arthritis, those close to him say he moved in and out of senility. His drinking had also worsened. Though it had been a problem for some time, it reportedly got worse. A gourmet food and wine connoisseur, Hitch's weight peaked at roughly 290 pounds, though he tried to keep it down by dieting to about 220 pounds. He avoided exercise. "In my case, I believe the overweight to be hereditary," he once said. "My mother, who lived to be 71, had what she called in England, 'a cottage-loaf figure."

While the alcohol and food perhaps helped numb the pain of arthritis, they exacerbated the problem with his weight. His roughly five-foot-seven frame carried an extra hundred pounds. Though he had trimmed down in the past, in the last years he ballooned back in size and found it hard to keep the weight off. "I think also that I gain weight because of my placid temperament," he said. "I simply never have a row." He also suffered from hypertension, a heart condition, and kidney problems.

He was aware the end was near, even if Alma wasn't. Alma, suffering from her own illnesses, was confined to a wheelchair and required around-the-clock medical care. Those close to the Hitchcocks said she too suffered from senility and was often "adrift from reality."

In January of 1980, he was knighted Commander of the British Empire by Queen Elizabeth. The announcement of the honor was actually made over Christmas 1979, at about the same time he was named Man of the Year by the British-American Chamber of Commerce. With his health frail, the ceremony took place at Universal Studios. Even though Hitchcock had officially retired from Universal, and his offices there had been dismantled, the event was held on a "set" created to give the appearance that Hitchcock was just having a "usual day at the office."

Hitchcock even rose to the occasion and spoke to the press of the knighthood. "I suppose it shows that if you stick at something long enough eventually somebody takes note." When asked if he thought it would make his wife treat him differently now that he was Sir Alfred Hitchcock, he joked, "I certainly hope so. Perhaps she will now mind her own business and do what she's told."

Even in the waning months of his life, Hitch still loved his stories and anecdotes and kept thinking there was still work to be done. There was a script, or stories that held promise of a potential film, and there were memories of the past, chatter about those he had worked with and scenes he captured for his cinematic creations. Though, those who spent time with him say he could be "slow and meandering in his storytelling, in no hurry to get anywhere."

A luncheon to celebrate his knighthood was held one afternoon and Cary Grant and Janet Leigh were among those who attended and once again honored the icon.

His last public appearance was in March 1980 when he was escorted to the Beverly Hilton Hotel to announce the recipient of the next American Film Institute Lifetime Achievement Award. It was customary for the previous year's recipient to announce the next one. In this instance it was especially poignant – the recipient was James Stewart. So

Hitchcock gathered up his strength and taped his opening remarks to be delivered at the ceremony. Though ill health prevented him from attending the actual event.

As April progressed, doctor visits to his home grew more and more frequent as his health declined, and his wife's health also suffered. On the evening of April 28, his family and those closest to him gathered. Doctors knew that the end was near. On April 29, 1980, at 9:17 a.m., Alfred Hitchcock died of kidney failure in his Los Angeles home at the age of 80.

His wife Alma would die two years later at the age of 82. However, after her husband's passing she was rarely aware he was gone. When visitors came to see her she would often say Hitch was "in the next room" or "at the studio."

A frugal man during his lifetime, possibly due to his upbringing, he wasn't known for a lavish lifestyle. While he enjoyed travel, good food and good wine, they were often expensed for business purposes. He was not known for extravagant spending on expensive cars, yachts or other trappings Hollywood's elite is known for. "I never want to risk anything," was something his daughter Patricia recalled him saying.

At the time of his death in 1980, he left an estate rich in stocks and bonds, along with his valuable California estate. Hitchcock owned more than two hundred thousand shares in MCA Universal, which made him one of the largest shareholders in the company. Aside from a wine cellar that held two cases of an 1875 Mouton-Rothschild and several cases of a 1921 Cheval-Blanc, the Hitchcocks did not live lavishly. His most valuable of possessions, though, came in his work.

While his entire legacy of film was considerable, five of his most famous films were entirely owned by Hitchcock and became the cornerstone of his wealthy estate – an estate worth an estimated $20 million at the time of his death.

The films included two that could likely be called two of the best he ever directed, *Rear Window* and *Vertigo*. A third film, *The Trouble With Harry*, was considered one of his personal favorites. The remaining two, *Rope* and *The Man Who Knew Too Much*, would represent two of the master's most challenging efforts.

In the 1970s he removed the films from circulation, ordering that all the prints be destroyed, and locking his original prints away for safekeeping. Several had not been seen since the 1960s, and would remain in hiding until after his death, when Universal bought worldwide rights to the classics for some $6 million. While the sum seemed extravagant at the time, it would prove to be a wise investment for Universal. With television and cable viewing, video releases, special editions, DVD and Blu-Ray copies, as well as theatrical re-releases, these films have continued to find new audiences and create new revenue streams for the studio. They also continue to keep the legacy of Alfred Hitchcock very much alive.

THE LOST HITCHCOCKS

THE LOST HITCHCOCKS

nineteen

THE LOST HITCHCOCKS

"The reportage of a news item in a newspaper will never have the impact of a moving picture. Catastrophe only happens to others, to people we don't know. The screen allows you to meet and to know the killer and his victim, for whom you're going to tremble with fear because you care about him."

- Alfred Hitchcock

The Path Not Chosen

While there are many films Hitchcock considered during the course of his career, the majority would be based on novels or short stories, or even newspaper clippings that got the director's juices flowing. Many would occupy a few hours or days of his time and he would abandon them for another idea that held more promise. Other projects would come in the form of screenplays, ready to go before the cameras, that Hitchcock would be offered, but turn down, preferring rather to go in another direction.

Here are a handful of noteworthy projects the director considered, but ultimately declined to move ahead with. These films would all eventually reach completion, realized by another director.

Anastasia

Alfred Hitchcock turned down the opportunity to direct the fact-based drama about a mysterious imposter posing as the Grand Duchess descended from Russian royalty. Starring Ingrid Bergman and Helen Hayes, Anatol Litvak would direct the completed film in 1956.

The Bad Seed

Hitchcock rejected the opportunity to make the film version of Maxwell Anderson's hit Broadway play about a monstrous little girl and her mother. Mervyn Leroy would direct the completed film in 1956.

Casino Royale

Hitchcock reportedly turned down the opportunity to acquire Ian Fleming's 1953 novel *Casino Royale,* featuring James Bond. First produced as a teleplay for TV in 1954, the story would later be treated as a spoof movie in 1967. Martin Campbell would direct the completed film.

Cleopatra

Producer Walter Wanger originally had Alfred Hitchcock in mind to direct a big screen version of *Cleopatra*. Wanger thought with Hitchcock in the director's chair the film would new deliver elements of suspense from the classic tale. Hitchcock rejected the idea. Joseph L. Mankiewicz would direct the completed 1963 film.

THE LOST HITCHCOCKS

Deathtrap
Alfred Hitchcock considered Ira Levin's 1978 hit stage thriller *Deathtrap*, but ultimately rejected the idea of filming a big screen version. Hitchcock screenwriter Jay Presson Allen adapted the play into a film and Sidney Lumet would direct the completed picture instead.

The Exorcist
Hitchcock turned down the opportunity to purchase the screen rights to William Peter Blatty's novel first, and then later turned down the offer to direct the feature film when another producer bought the rights to the story. William Friedkin would direct the completed 1973 hit film.

Jane Eyre
The director turned down an offer for him to direct a feature film version of Charlotte Bronte's classic Gothic novel. Robert Stevenson would direct the completed film in 1944.

The Keys of the Kingdom
Hitchcock liked A.J. Cronin's novel about a young priest sent to establish a Catholic parish in China, but plans for him to direct a big screen version fell through. John M. Stahl would direct the 1944 completed film.

No Highway in the Sky
Even with James Stewart as its star, Hitchcock turned down the opportunity to direct this thriller, based on a novel by Nevil Shute about an aeronautical engineer who believes the crowded plane he is on will fall apart during its flight. Henry Koster directed the completed film in 1951.

Rosemary's Baby
Hitchcock reportedly turned down the chance to acquire Ira Levin's novel, *Rosemary's Baby*, leaving open the chance for B-movie maker, William Castle to secure the rights. When Paramount rejected the idea of Castle directing, they again wanted Hitchcock. However, Hitchcock

again passed on the idea. Roman Polanski would direct the completed 1968 film.

Sleuth
Hitchcock turned down directing duties for the movie version of Anthony Shaffer's hit play *Sleuth*. Joseph L. Mankiewicz would direct the completed 1972 film.

The Spiral Staircase
Alfred Hitchcock couldn't sell himself on the tale of a handicapped young woman in turn-of-the-century New England, being terrorized by a serial killer who preys on handicapped women. Robert Siodmak would direct the completed film in 1945.

Wait Until Dark
Hitchcock was offered a chance to purchase the screen rights to the hit Broadway play *Wait Until Dark* by Frederick Knott. Knott was the writer of *Dial 'M' For Murder*, previously made into a film by Hitchcock. Terence Young would direct the completed film, released in 1967 starring Audrey Hepburn.

What Ever Happened to Baby Jane?
When producer William Frye considered taking an option on William Farrell's novel in 1960, he and his friend, Bette Davis tried to convince Hitchcock to direct Davis and Joan Crawford in the film version. He declined because he was too busy with the international release of *Psycho* and was already developing the screenplay for his next film, *The Birds*. Robert Aldrich would direct the completed film, released in 1962.

A Woman's Face
Hitchcock, under contract to producer David O. Selznick, wanted to be loaned out to MGM for this dark tale of a scarred woman trying to overcome her troubled past. It would star Joan Crawford. George Cukor

would direct the completed 1941 film.

The Devil's Disciple

George Bernard Shaw's play was to have been Hitchcock's follow-up film after *Foreign Correspondent*. However, Shaw refused to release the film rights because it was a satire about America and England during the Revolutionary War. He felt it inappropriate to be filmed while America and England were allied in the fight against Nazi Germany. Hitchcock made *Mr. and Mrs. Smith* instead. *The Devil's Disciple* was eventually made into a film in 1959 in collaboration between Burt Lancaster and Kirk Douglas.

Malice Aforethought

Hitchcock's film *Suspicion* was based on a novel by Francis Iles called *Before the Fact*. Around 1945 Hitchcock wanted to adapt another novel by the same author. Iles was actually a pseudonym used by journalist Anthony Berkeley. *Malice Aforethought* was one of the first "inverted" mysteries, where the identity of the criminal is known at the start. Rather than a "whodunit," the audience watches to see if the killer gets away with it, or how he gets caught. About a doctor who murders his wife, Hitchcock didn't think he could get a major star actor to take on the lead role of a killer. *Malice Aforethought* would eventually be made into a TV series by the BBC in 1979.

THE LOST HITCHCOCKS

THE LOST HITCHCOCKS

twenty

THE LOST HITCHCOCKS

"I'm full of fears and I do my best to avoid difficulties and any kind of complications. I like everything around me to be clear as crystal and completely calm."

- Alfred Hitchcock

Closing Remarks

Much has been written about Alfred Hitchcock. He was both a fascinating and puzzling man, professionally and personally. Writer and filmmaker Francois Truffaut once remarked, "Hitchcock revels in being misunderstood, more so because it is on misunderstandings that he has constructed his life."

The statement perhaps helps explain why the public has endured such a long, and at times, complex love affair with the man. One biographer suggested that, "he's a man who always looks like he just come from a funeral," describing him with his "rotund Santa Claus like body," always dressed in a "navy blue suit, white shirt, and banker's tie."

Beneath the unassuming and unthreatening appearance was a complicated man whose humor could be risqué, dark, droll, dry and often fraught with innuendo. He was fascinated by both sex and murder. His complete work stands testament to the gruesomeness of life and the macabre behavior of the everyday man. It was if he was saying "yes, I'm fascinated by this, but you are too," or "you're an accomplice for being as fascinated by it as I am."

As talented and brilliant as Hitchcock was, he was also a man who was clearly flawed. Consumed with insecurities, he could also be self-absorbed and self-obsessed. Actress Anne Baxter one told a story that, during the making of *I Confess,* she invited Alma Hitchcock out for a drive and lunch in the country. Alma excitedly agreed, but made it clear she needed to be back to the city by the dinner hour. Baxter recalled that New York traffic made their commute back longer than expected and she could sense Alma's growing anxiety as the delay increased. The two were nearly an hour late by the time they arrived back at the hotel, where Hitchcock was waiting for his wife for dinner. "He was a patient ball of anger and desperation," Baxter noted. Dependent on his wife, Alma was a mass of nerves, knowing he was waiting for her. She passed it off with a joke, but Hitchcock was not interested. His dinner hour was set and he expected her to be there. Baxter said that Hitchcock was angry with her for years after that incident, holding her personally responsible for ruining his evening.

Though Hitchcock was angry with Alma for displeasing him, it was because he was so immensely dependent on her. Those who worked with Hitchcock noted that Hitch was rare to ever compliment anyone for their work or performance. Actors, writers and members of his film crew would say Hitchcock rarely or never offered praise. However, one way he would offer the rare compliment was to say Alma liked something.

Screenwriter John Michael Hayes, who worked with Hitchcock on four films commented, "I knew that he liked the script when he told me Alma liked it - that was the only way he could offer a compliment."

Hayes was one of the many collaborators who worked with Hitchcock, and many would claim he preferred being alone in the spotlight, often ignoring the fact that others played key roles in his successes. He would take credit for the films, the performances, television episodes, even the articles in magazines that bared his name. In many cases, he had little role in episodes of his series or the short stories in his books or magazines, but he knew it was his name and likeness that drew in the public, and he was happy to accept the praise, even if he himself found it difficult to give.

He could also be terribly self-centered. While he made millions off his face and name, he often went out of his way to deny others any profit from the success of working with him. He would always refuse to use his name when acquiring works for his pictures. His agents would never mention Hitchcock when negotiating the price of a book or play. Films like *Strangers on a Train* and *Psycho* were purchased at bargain prices because the authors had no idea they would become Hitchcock pictures, and actors like Vera Miles and Tippi Hedren were initially approached about working for Hitch by others, without mention of his name. Even writers like John Michael Hayes and Evan Hunter would say Hitchcock paid them very little for their services. He seemed to feel that the honor of working with him should be enough. But writers would often end up parting ways with Hitchcock over money. For Hayes the final straw came when Hitchcock wanted him to write a screenplay for free. The director had promised Warner Bros. a free picture, as part of a multi-picture deal and when it came time to make the film, *The Wrong Man*, Hitch felt if he was to work for free, so should his screenwriter. Hayes, who had a family, and recalled making roughly only $75,000 - before taxes - over four films and several years working for the director, said no and their relationship ended a short time later.

Others would find Hitch punishing. He would deny Vera Miles

opportunities to work when she chose marriage and children over a chance to appear in *Vertigo*. He would behave similarly with Tippi Hedren, years later when she refused his advances and he would attempt to ruin her by not allowing her to work because he held a contract with her and refused to use her. He wouldn't even attend Grace Kelly's Monaco wedding because he saw her abandoning him for the role of a princess instead of his star. However, when it came time to pay tribute to his life and career, not long before his death, they all turned out to pay tribute to the man.

He once said, "If I made *Cinderella*, the audience would start looking for the body in the pumpkin coach." He went on to assume, "If an audience sees one of my productions with no spine-tingling, they're disappointed." And he was right, we were.

His films still earn acclaim and attention – and money. In 1998, when the American Film Institute (AFI) released its list of the 100 greatest movies of all time, Hitchcock hit the list four times. The films were judged on a variety of criteria, including their cultural impact, historical significance, popularity and awards, and critical recognition, among others. Three of his films landed in the top 50. *Vertigo* came in at 61 on the list, while *Rear Window* appeared at 42. *North by Northwest* made it to number 40, and his 1960 classic *Psycho* came in at 18. He should have made the top ten, but Hitchcock was denied an Academy Award as best director, even with five nominations. So the judging criteria affected his ultimate place in the AFI history books.

He was first nominated for an Academy Award for *Rebecca*, and although the film would go on to earn best picture, surprisingly enough, he was not awarded a statuette. John Ford took the award for *Grapes of Wrath* instead. He was nominated again for *Lifeboat* in 1944, but would lose to Leo McCary and that year's best picture, *Going My Way*.

Two years later, in 1946, he would again be nominated, this time for *Spellbound*. However, he lost the award to Billy Wilder, who took home best director and best picture for statues for *The Lost Weekend*.

In 1955, when *On The Waterfront* took 1954's best picture, it also came away with a best director award for its director Elia Kazan and Hitchcock again lost out when he was nominated for *Rear Window*. At last, in 1961, many thought it would be the director's moment to shine. He once again found his work nominated when *Psycho* earned him recognition for the best director award. However, he would lose again, this time to Billy Wilder, whose best picture and best director win for *The Apartment* would deny Hitchcock his last chance at winning an Oscar.

In 1967 The Academy of Motion Pictures Arts and Sciences would attempt to right its wrong by honoring Hitchcock with its Irving Thalberg Award. The Award is presented to filmmakers whose impressive credentials are considered long overdue for formal recognition by the Academy. Such was certainly the case when Hitchcock received the award for his body of work. It was a welcome moment, as his recent films, *Marnie* and *Torn Curtain,* had not fared well with the critics or with moviegoers.

Since then his work has continued to astound moviegoers and his life and career have been evaluated and re-evaluated. Some writers have glossed over Hitchcock's later years, suggesting his work after *Psycho* was merely a downward spiral, but those assessments miss the mark. As a seasoned filmmaker, Hitchcock was evaluated on a standard above many others. His later films offer glimpses of greatness and continue to reward with repeated viewings. Those films are still being re-evaluated within the scope of his entire career.

While Hitchcock was certainly not without his flaws, his cinematic achievements are beyond impressive. His treatment of his actors, including a number of his leading ladies was less than perfect, and at times downright harassment, but what he and his collaborators left on celluloid offer us cinematic gems.

Countless films have been reviewed with the words, "what might Hitchcock have done," and even more are still promoted as "Hitchcockian" in their suspense. Yet, without Hitchcock at the helm, they are mere copies of a style of filmmaking, without the filmmaker. Of the many films he left on the table, having never completed, we're left to wonder what might have been.

Even so, considering Hitchcock's Hollywood films, from *Rebecca* through *Family Plot*, it's estimated that Hitchcock's work grossed more than $223 million. It's an impressive amount when one considers tickets prices at movie houses for many of the years he was releasing films was less than 50 cents and even by 1976, when his final film was released, the average ticket was less than $2.50.

Still they keep on earning. DVD and Blu-Ray releases and theatrical re-releases of his films still garner attention. He is still one of the most recognizable names and faces in Hollywood's long and illustrious history. As a director, he made more than 50 motion pictures. He once said he only made one mystery film and he wanted viewers to understand the difference between mystery and suspense.

"Mystery is mystifying; it is an intellectual thing. Suspense is an emotional thing. The audience does not necessarily emote when it is mystified, but it does emote with suspense. The point is to give the viewers information which the cast doesn't have. If you see a man with a club coming up behind an innocent person, you know more than the innocent person does, and suspense is created."

Appendix

THE LOST HITCHCOCKS

THE LOST HITCHCOCKS

"I'm aware that you and many other critics feel that all of my films resemble one another. But to me, strangely enough, every film is a brand-new thing."

Alfred Hitchcock

Filmography

The Films of Alfred Hitchcock in reverse chronological order.

1970s

- Family Plot (1976)

- Frenzy (1972)

1960s

- Topaz (1969)
- Torn Curtain (1966)
- Marnie (1964)
- The Birds (1963)
- "The Alfred Hitchcock Hour" (1 episode, 1962)
- "Alfred Hitchcock Presents" (17 episodes, 1955-1961)
- Psycho (1960)
- "Ford Star Time" (1 episode, 1960)

1950s

- North by Northwest (1959)
- Vertigo (1958)
- "Suspicion" (1 episode, 1957)
- The Wrong Man (1956)
- The Man Who Knew Too Much (1956)

- The Trouble with Harry (1955)
- To Catch a Thief (1955)
- Rear Window (1954)
- Dial M For Murder (1954)
- I Confess (1953)
- Strangers on a Train (1951)
- Stage Fright (1950)

1940s

- Under Capricorn (1949)
- Rope (1948)
- The Paradine Case (1947)
- Notorious (1946)
- Spellbound (1945)
- Watchtower Over Tomorrow (1945) (uncredited)
- The Fighting Generation (1944) (uncredited)
- Lifeboat (1944)

- Aventure malgache (1944)
- Bon Voyage (1944)
- Shadow of a Doubt (1943)
- Saboteur (1942)
- Suspicion (1941)
- Mr. & Mrs. Smith (1941)
- Foreign Correspondent (1940)
- Rebecca (1940)

1930s

- Jamaica Inn (1939)
- The Lady Vanishes (1938)
- Young and Innocent (1937)
- Sabotage (1936)
- Secret Agent (1936)
- The 39 Steps (1935)

- The Man Who Knew Too Much (1934)
- Waltzes from Vienna (1934)
- Number Seventeen (1932)
- Rich and Strange (1931)
- Mary (1931)
- The Skin Game (1931)
- Murder! (1930)
- Juno and the Paycock (1930)
- An Elastic Affair (1930)
- Elstree Calling (1930) (provided sketches)

1920s

- The Manxman (1929)
- Blackmail (1929)
- Champagne (1928)
- Easy Virtue (1928)
- The Farmer's Wife (1928)

THE LOST HITCHCOCKS

- Downhill (1927)

- The Ring (1927)

- The Lodger: A Story of the London Fog (1927)

- The Mountain Eagle (1926)

- The Pleasure Garden (1925)

- Always Tell Your Wife (1923) (uncredited)

- Number 13 (1922) (unfinished)

THE LOST HITCHCOCKS

Sources

THE LOST HITCHCOCKS

"I have great respect for crime and the people involved with it, and such being the case, I deplore the careless crime. It has no finesse, no sense of balance, no feeling of accomplishment."

Alfred Hitchcock

Bibliography

Selected Bibliography

A number of books, magazines, newspapers, documentaries and interviews, as well as the films themselves provided sources of information and factual data that went into the writing of this book. Thank you to the many sources referenced throughout the book. There were many individuals whose work, insights, reviews, comments and suggestions that also helped make this book possible.

Books

Aulier, Dan. "Htichcock's Notebooks. 1999. Avon Books.

Campbell, Robert. The Golden Years of Broadcasting. 1976. New York. Rutledge Books.

Finler, Joel W. The Hollywood Story. 1988. New York. Crown Publishers, Inc.

Harris, Robert A., Lasky, Michael S. The Films of Alfred Hitchcock. 1976. New York. Citadel Press.

Hingham, Charles. Audrey - The Life of Audrey Hepburn. 1984. Macmillan Publishing Company.

Hirschhorn, Clive. The Universal Story. 1983. New York. Crown Publishers, Inc.

Humphries, Patrick. The Films of Alfred Hitchcock. 1986. New Jersey. Crescent Books.

Hunter, Evan. Me and Hitch. 1997. London and Boston. Faber and Faber

Jones, Stephen. Clive Barker's A-Z of Horror. 1997. New York. HarperPrism.

Kapsis, Robert E. Hitchcock: The Making of a Reputation. 1992. Chicago. The University of Chicago Press.

Kraft, Jeff and Leventhal, Aaron. Footsteps in the Fog. 2002. Santa Monica Press.

Leigh, Janet. Psycho – Behind the Scenes of the Classic Thriller. 1996. New York. Harmony Books.

McCarty, John. The Fearmakers. 1994. New York. St. Martin's Press.

McCarty, John. The Modern Horror Film. 1990. New York. Citadel Press.

McCarty, John. Psychos – Eighty Years of Mad Movies, Maniacs, and Murderous Deeds. 1986. New York. St Martin's Press.

Moog, Ken. The Alfred Hitchcock Story. 1999. London. Titan Books. Nelson, Nancy. Evenings with Cary Grant. 1991. New York. Warner Books.

Osteen, Mark. Hitchcock and Adaptation - On the Page and The Screen. 2014. Lanham, Maryland. Roman and Littlefield

Quirk, Lawrence. The Films of Paul Newman. 1971. New Jersey. Citadel Press.

Schoell, Willam. Stay Out of the Shower – 25 Years of Shocker Films Beginning with 'Psycho.' 1985. New York. Dembner Books.

Shulman, Arthur & Youman, Roger. How Sweet It Was. 1966. New York. Bonanza Books.

Spoto, Donald. The Dark Side of Genius: The Life of Alfred Hitchcock. 1983. New York. Ballantine Books.

Spoto, Donald. The Art of Alfred Hitchcock. 1992. New York. Anchor Books.

Sternfield, Jonathan. The Look of Horror – Scary Moments from Scary Movies. 1990. Philadelphia. M&M Books.

Sterritt, David. The Films of Alfred Hitchcock. 1993. New York. Cambridge University Press.

Stirling, Richard. Julie Andrews – An Intimate Biography. 2007. New York. St. Martin's Press.

Magazines, Newspapers

Aitken, Mark. "The Day Connery's 007 Career Nearly Went for a Burton." Daily Mail. August 26, 2006.

Camp, Joyce. "John Buchan and Alfred Hitchcock." Literature Film Quarterly. Summer 1978.

Coburn, Robert. "Fine Feathered Friends on a Rampage." Life Magazine. February 1, 1963.

Craft, Dan. "Diabolique." The Patangraph. August 15, 1997.

Curtis, Quentin. "Hitchcock the Romantic: His Films Famously Celebrated and Tortured Women." The Daily Telegraph." April 27, 1996.

Davis, Ivor. "Return of the Missing Hitchcock's." The Times. November 15, 1983.

Freeman, David. "Alfred Hitchcock's Fade to Black: The Great Director's Final Days." The Daily Beast. December 13, 2014.

Goodman, Erza. "Mysterious Mr. Hitchcock." Cinema Progress. Volume 3, Issue 2, 1938.

Higham, Charles. "Hitchcock's World." Film Quarterly. December 1, 1962.

Kerh, Dave. "Marnie." The Chicago Tribune. October 23, 1986.

La Bern, Arthur. "Letters to the Editor: Hitchcock's 'Frenzy.'" The Times of London. May 29, 1972.

Liston, Enjoli. "Hollyweird – Alfred Hitchcock and Steven Spielberg." The Independent. October 2, 2009.

Lowrance, Dee. "Movieland's Spy Master." Montana Standard. November 8, 1942.

McCarthy, Todd. "Alfred Hitchcock Dies of Natural Causes at Bel-Air Home." Variety. April 30, 1980.

Miller, Ron. "A Cool Blond Looks Back." The Chicago Tribune. March 24, 1994.

Morton, Tony. "She's at Home at the Zoo." Omaha World Herald. May 21, 1995.

Smith, Graham. "Revealed: The secret telegram that shows Ian Fleming wanted Alfred Hitchcock to direct the first Bond film." DailyMail.com. May 15, 2012.

Staff. "Anxiety The Secret." Aberdeen Evening Express. November 18, 1952.

Staff. "Filming Hamlet." Aberdeen Journal. September 5, 1945.

Staff. "Titanic Almost His." Brooklyn Daily Eagle. August 13, 2008.

Staff. "Hitchcock to Direct Three American Films." Dundee Evening Telegraph. March 17, 1939.

Staff. "Hitchcock Lives Quiet Life." Lethbridge Herald. March 16, 1971.

Thomas, Bob and Hitchcock, Alfred. "Interview with Alfred Hitchcock." Action Journal, Directors Guild of America. 1968

Thomas, Bob. "Alfred Hitchcock is 75, Busy Directing New Movie." Anniston Star. August 25, 1975.

Thomas, Bob. "Hollywood." Associated Press. August 6, 1979.

Wilkinson, Lupton A. "He Makes the Movies Move." Los Angeles Times. January 5, 1941.

Williams, J. Danvers. "What I'd Do to the Stars." Film Weekly. March 4, 1939.

Internet Sources

Additional sources for comfirming or supplementing research:

The Alfred Hitchcock Wiki: www.hitchcockwiki.com

Wikipedia: www.wikipedia.com

The Internet Movie Database: www.imdb.com

The Numbers – Box Office Data, Movie Stars, Idle Speculation: www.the-numbers.com

Box Office Mojo: www.boxofficemojo.com

Photographic Credits

In addition to the selected bibliograpy of sources we would also like to acknowledge the many photographs used in this book. While many are part of the author's private collection, we would like to specifically acknowledge the following for illustrations used that are used for the purpose of review to highlight and complement the text:

Alfred Hitchcock Productions; Shamley Productions, Inc.; 20th Century Fox; United Artists, Universal; Paramount Pictures, Sipa Press; Life Magazine; Cinema Photos; CinemaShop.

Index

THE LOST HITCHCOCKS

Index

Symbols

39 Steps, The 61, 62, 64, 180, 181, 247

A

Aberdeen Journal 88
Academy Award 32, 48, 54, 104, 135, 182, 238
Academy of Motion Picture Arts and Sciences 191, 197
Aldrich, Robert 230
Alfred Hitchcock Hour, The 34, 245
Alfred Hitchcock Presents 33, 73, 103, 104, 115, 116, 129, 136, 188, 245
Allen, Irwin 1, 268
Allen, Jay Presson 148, 229
Ambler, Eric 107, 125
American Film Institute 204, 221, 238
Anastasia 228
Anderson, Michael 107
Andrea Doria 77
Andrews, Julie 170, 183, 188, 255
Annie Get Your Gun 103

Anthony Hopkins 22
Antonioni, Michelangelo 192
A Nun's Story 113, 118
Archibald, William 96
Arthur 116
Ault, Marie 52
Awful Truth, The 86
A Woman's Face 65, 66, 230

B

Bad Seed, The 228
BAFTA 22
Balcon, Michael 53
Banco's Chair 115
Bantam 205
Barrie, James M. 146
Bates Motel 23
Baxter, Anne 236
BBC 22, 231
Before the Fact 66, 231
Bell, Book and Candle 135
Benchley, Peter 202, 204
Bergman, Ingrid 62, 64, 188, 228
Bernstein, Sidney 83, 86, 87
Birds, The 16, 23, 34, 69, 130, 141, 148, 150, 161, 162, 164, 167, 168, 182, 194, 197, 204, 206, 212, 230, 245
Blake, George 212
Blatty, William Peter 229
Bloch, Robert 119, 193
Blonde Venus 85
Blow Up 192
Bob Pender Stage Troupe 85
Bogart, Humphrey 113
Bond, James 123, 124, 125, 126, 128, 129, 130
Boy and the Bridge, The 125
Bramble Bush, The 91–269
Bristol-Meyers 34
Broccoli, Albert 123, 124, 127, 128
Bronte, Charlotte 229
Brown, Katharine 43
Bryce, Ivar 125, 126
Buchan, John 61, 62, 65, 179, 180, 181, 182, 255
Bumstead, Henry 115
Burkes, Robert 193

Burton, Richard 98
Butterfield 8 115
Bwana Devil 98

C

Callas, Maria 138
Campbell, Martin 228
Cannes Film Festival 167
Capra, Frank 64
Carroll, Madeleine 61
Carson, Jack 98
Casino Royale 129, 228
Castle, William 229
CBS 34, 73, 129
Cecil, Henry 116
Charade 119
Chasens 91, 92
Chesney, Arthur 52
Cinema According to Hitchcock 23
Citizen Kane 22
Cleopatra 228
Coleman, Herbert 75, 76, 115
Columbia 66, 85, 98
Compton, Fay 146, 148
Connery, Sean 128, 130, 161, 170, 213, 255
Cooper, Gary 103, 104, 107
Crawford, Joan 65, 230
Cukor, George 230
Cunard 43
Cunard Line 42

D

Dante 82
Davis, Bette 230
Day, Doris 72
Deathtrap 229
Defoe 82
D'Entre les Mortes 73, 76, 77
Dern, Bruce 203
Devil's Disciple, The 231
Dial M for Murder 33
Dial M For Murder 96, 98, 115, 194, 246
Dickens, Charles 82
Dickinson, Angie 98

Dick Powell Show, The 148
Dietrich, Marlene 85
Disney, Walt 139, 140, 141
Disneyland 139, 140
Donat 62
Donat, Robert 61, 62, 64, 181
Douglas, Kirk 231
Drake, Betsy 77
Dreyfuss, Richard 207
Dr. No 124, 128, 129
Du Maurier, Daphne 41
Duncan, David 94
DuPont Show of the Month, The 148

E

Eastwood, Clint 213
Ed Sullivan Show, The 33
Eliot, T.S. 181
Emmy Award 33
Eon Productions 123
Erickson, Doc 75
Exorcist, The 229

F

Fairbanks, Douglas 40
Family Plot 34, 173, 176, 203, 208, 211, 212, 240, 244
Famous Players Film Company 71
Famous Players Lasky 40
Film Weekly 47, 257
Flamingo Feather 69–269
Fleming, Ian 123, 124, 125, 126, 128, 129, 228, 257
Flight to Egypt 95
Fonda, Henry 103, 137
Ford, John 48, 137, 238
Foreign Correspondent 58, 64, 103, 206, 231, 247
Frenzy 34, 69, 174, 193, 197, 203, 244, 256
Friedkin, William 229
Frohman, Charles 71
Frohman, Daniel 71
Frye, William 230

G

Gavin, John 168
Geraghty, Tom 40

Girl, The 22
Going My Way. 238
Golden Globe 22
Goldwyn, Samuel 45
Gone With the Wind 44, 45
Grant, Cary 57, 62, 64, 75, 77, 83, 84, 85, 86, 88, 115, 119, 126, 135, 137, 153, 168, 192, 221, 254
Grapes of Wrath, The 48, 238
Green, Hilton 215
Greenmantle 61, 62, 64, 65, 66
Griswold, Claire 148, 150
Gunzberg, M.I. 98

H

Haigh, John George 193
Hall, Mordant 40
Hamlet 11–269, 81–269, 83–269, 84–269, 85–269, 86–269, 87–269, 88–269, 257–269
Harbraugh, Carl 41
Harrison, Joan 46, 125, 183
Harvey, Laurence 114, 115, 116
Hayes, Helen 228
Hayes, John Michael 73, 237
HBO 22
Head, Edith 183
Hedren, Tippi 22, 146, 148, 149, 161, 162, 167, 168, 170, 237, 238
Hepburn, Audrey 111, 112, 113, 115, 116, 117, 118, 119, 150, 230, 253
Herrmann, Bernard 104
Heston, Charlton 107
His Girl Friday 86
Hitchcock, Alma 32, 43, 75, 77, 92, 93, 96, 197, 220, 222, 236, 237
Hitchcock, Emma 31
Hitchcock (FIlm) 22
Hitchcock, Nellie 77
Hitchcock's Monster Movie 16, 23
Hitchcock/Truffaut 23
Hitchcock, William 31
Hodder & Stoughton 62
Hodkinson, W.W. 71
Holden, William 113
Hopkins, Anthony 22
House of Wax 98
How to Steal a Million 119
Hunter, Evan 237

I

Iles, Francis 231
I'm No Angel 85
Innes, Hammond 102
Inn of the Sixth Happiness, The 181
I Confess 69, 94, 96, 194, 236, 246
Iwerks, Ub 141

J

Jamaica Inn 39, 46, 247
Jane Eyre 229
Jaws 201–269

K

Kaleidoscope 187–269
Kazan, Elia 239
Keen, Malcolm 52
Kelly, Grace 74, 75, 118, 148, 150, 238
Keon, Barbara 96
Knott, Frederick 230
Koster, Henry 229
Krim, Arthur 127

L

Lady Vanishes, The 39, 43, 247
Lancaster, Burt 231
Lasky Feature Play Compan 71
Lawrence of Arabia 62
Lawrence, T. E. 62
Lehman, Ernest 104, 105, 106, 117, 137, 138, 139, 140, 213, 214
Leigh, Janet 155, 156, 188, 221, 254
Leroy, Mervin 228
Leviathan 42, 46
Levin, Ira 229
Levy, Benn 193
Lifeboat 32, 48, 206, 238, 246
Litvak, Anatol 228
Lloyd, Norman 214
Lodger, The 11, 51, 51–269, 52, 53, 54, 55, 57, 58, 249
Longfellow 82
Lord Camber's Ladies 193
Los Angeles County Museum of Modern Art 204
Los Angeles Times 46, 257

Lost Weekend, The 238
Lowndes, Marie Belloc 51
Lucy 33
Lumet, Sidney 229

M

Malice Aforethought 231
Manchurian Candidate, The 115
Man in the Dark 98
Mankiewicz, Joseph L. 228, 230
Man Who Shot Liberty Valance, The 137
Margaret Herrick Library 197
Marie Celeste, The 106
Marnie 11, 34, 130, 148, 150, 161, 167, 169, 170, 192, 194, 197, 203, 239, 245, 256
Mary Rose 145–269
Matthau, Walter 213
MCA 126, 127, 128, 222
McCary, Leo 238
McClory, Kevin 125, 126, 127, 128
MGM 45, 65, 66, 86, 103, 104, 105, 106, 107, 230
Miles, Vera 118, 150, 158, 237
Mitchell, Margaret 44
Mizner, Wilson 41
Mr. and Mrs. Smith 66, 231
Mr. Standfast, 62
MS Stockholm 77
Murder in the Cathedral 181
Mutiny on the Bounty 45
My Favorite Wife 86

N

NBC 34
Newman, Paul 170, 183, 188, 206, 207, 254
New York Times 40, 44
No Highway in the Sky 229
None but the Lonely Heart 83
North by Northwest 33, 34, 73, 106, 107, 114, 118, 126, 153, 183, 194, 238, 245
Novak, Kim 135
No Bail for the Judge 111–269
Novello, Ivor 52, 53, 54

O

One Plus One Equals One 204

On The Waterfront 238
Original Sin 95
Orton, Jock 87
O'Shea, Dan 86

P

Paradine Case, The 33, 83, 115, 246
Paramount Studios 40, 45, 63, 71, 72, 73, 76, 93, 116, 117, 118, 119, 136, 229, 259
Peck, Gregory 57, 113
Perry Mason 148
Personal History 64
Petrie, Daniel 98
Philadelphia Story, The 86
Polanski, Roman 230
Prince Rainier of Monaco 75
Psycho 16, 22, 23, 34, 107, 119, 135, 136, 140, 150, 155, 157, 158, 159, 162, 171, 174, 182, 192, 193, 194, 196, 197, 204, 206, 208, 212, 230, 237, 238, 239, 245, 254

Q

Queen Elizabeth 221

R

Rainbird Pattern, The 204, 208
Rich and Strange 82, 248
Richards, Dick 207
RKO 45, 66, 83
Robertson, Peggy 137, 192
Roman, Ruth 77
Rope 94, 135, 222, 246
Rosemary's Baby 229
Rear Window 33, 71, 73, 135, 182, 192, 194, 204, 222, 238, 239, 246
Rebecca 32, 41, 47, 48, 54, 220, 238, 240, 247
Reville, Alma 32, 43, 75, 77, 92, 93, 96, 197, 220, 222, 236, 237
Roman Holiday 112
Room at the Top 115
Rush, Barbara 98

S

Saboteur 32, 214, 247
Sabrina 112, 115
Saltzman, Harry 123, 124, 127, 128

Schary, Dore 103
Schatz, Arthur 195
Scheider, Roy 207
Schochet, Stephen 203
Screen Producers Guild, The 150
Selznick, David O. 32, 39, 41, 42, 43, 44, 45, 46, 47, 48, 58, 64, 65, 66, 86, 230
Selznick International Pictures, 86
Seven Brides for Seven Brothers 103
Shadow of a Doubt 32, 247
Shaffer, Anthony 230
Shakespeare, William 82, 83, 85, 86, 88
Shamley Productions 34, 259
Shaw, George Bernard 231
She Done Him Wrong 85
Short Night, The 211–269
Shute, Nevil 229
Sight and Sound Magazine 21
Sinatra, Frank 115
Singin' in the Rain 103
Siodmak, Robert 230
Sleuth 230
South, Leonard 183
Spellbound 57, 182, 238, 246
Spielberg, Steven 201, 203, 256
Spiral Staircase, The 230
Stage Fright 33, 69, 94, 246
Stanwyck, Barbara 48
Stevenson, Robert 229
Stewart, James 71, 72, 74, 75, 76, 133, 134, 135, 137, 138, 140, 188, 221, 229
Sting, The 207
Strangers on a Train 33, 77, 94, 194, 237, 246
Sturges, John 207
Suspicion 32, 57, 66, 86, 231, 245, 247

T

Tabori, George 95, 96
Tales of Hollywood 203
Taylor, Rod 130, 168
Taylor, Samuel 115, 117
Technicolor 116
Thalberg, Irving 239
The Alfred Hitchcock Hour 245
The Birds 161, 162, 164, 167, 168, 245
The Blind Man 133–269

The Trouble with Harry 246
Thirty-Nine Steps, The 62
Three Hostages, The 179–269
Thunderball 123–269
Times of London, The 149, 256
Titanic 11, 39, 41, 42, 43, 44, 45, 46, 47, 48, 257
Tomasini, George 182, 183
Topaz 34, 196, 197, 212, 245
Topper 86
Torn Curtain 34, 170, 183, 187, 189, 191, 192, 194, 197, 206, 212, 239, 245
To Catch a Thief 246
Transatlantic Pictures 83, 84, 88, 94
Trap for a Solitary Man 140
Tripp, June 52
Trouble With Harry, The 73, 194, 222
Truffaut, Francios 23, 53, 55, 56, 57, 150, 151, 182, 191, 196, 235
Turn of the Screw, The 96
Twentieth-Century Fox 48, 65, 66
Twilight Zone, The 148
Two Rode Together 137

U

Ullman, Liv 213
Under Capricorn 33, 83, 88, 246
Unforgiven, The 113
United Artists 57, 64, 127, 259
Universal 16, 136, 150, 157, 158, 162, 171, 172, 173, 175, 182, 195, 196, 197, 203, 204, 206, 207, 208, 212, 215, 221, 222, 223, 253, 259

V

van der Post, Laurens 69, 72, 75
Variety 47, 72, 256
Vertigo 21, 33, 69, 77, 104, 117, 135, 158, 182, 194, 222, 238, 245
Village of Stars 141
VistaVision 116

W

Wait Until Dark 230
Wanger, Walter 57, 63, 64, 65, 66, 228
Warner Bros. 45, 65, 66, 71, 72, 73, 83, 94, 96, 97, 98, 103, 237
Warner, Jack 96
Wasserman, Lew 103, 126, 150, 195, 196
Wayne, John 137
Webb, Clifton 48

West, Mae 85
What Ever Happened to Baby Jane? 230
Whitlock, Albert 148
Whittingham, Jack 127
Wilder, Billy 238, 239
Williams, John 115, 116
Wreck of the Mary Deare 101–269
Wrong Man, The 33, 73, 75, 103, 158, 194, 237, 245
Wyman, Jane 94

X

Xanadu Productions 125

Y

Young, Terence 128, 230

Z

Zukor, Adolph 45, 71

THE LOST HITCHCOCKS

About the Author

John William Law is a writer and journalist whose work has appeared in newspapers, magazines and books. He has worked on the staffs of daily, weekly and monthly publications. He is the author of numerous books and narrates a podcast on iTunes entitled *Behind the Screen with The Movie Files*. He has appeared on television and film documentaries discussing film history and on national public radio. His 2010 book, *Alfred Hitchcock: The Icon Years* was named Best Non-Fiction title in the Readers Favorite Book Awards and in 2014 his book *Who Nuked The Duke?* was named Best Non-Fiction title at the San Francisco Book Festival. His 2016 book, *Movie Star & the Mobster*, won the London, New York and Hollywood Book Festivals for Best General Non-Fiction. He lives in San Francisco. His books include:

Curse of the Silver Screen - Tragedy & Disaster Behind the Movies (1999, Aplomb Publishing)

Scare Tactic - The Life and Films of William Castle (2000, Writers Club Press)

Reel Horror - True Horrors Behind Hollywood's Scary Movies (2004, Aplomb Publishing)

Alfred Hitchcock: The Icon Years (2010, Aplomb Publishing)

What Ever Happened to Mommie Dearest? (2012, Aplomb Publishing)

Who Nuked the Duke? (2014, Aplomb Publishing)

Movie Star & the Mobster (2016, Aplomb Publishing)

If you enjoyed this book, you might also enjoy *Movie Star & the Mobster*. Published by Aplomb Publishing, the book is available through our Web site at www.aplombpublishing.com or from major booksellers and Amazon.com, and an enhanced edition is available for Apple iBooks on iTunes.

www.ingramcontent.com/pod-product-compliance
Lightning Source LLC
Chambersburg PA
CBHW050122020526
44112CB00035B/2248